Smashing *through* Death's Door

by Marshall J. Alexander

as told to Trish Ramos

BRIDGE
LOGOS
FOUNDATION

Alachua, Florida 32615

Bridge-Logos
Alachua, FL 32615 USA

Smashing Through Death's Door
by Marshall J. Alexander

Edited by Trish Ramos

Copyright ©2010 by Bridge-Logos

Printed in the United States of America.

Library of Congress Catalog Card Number: 2010924415
International Standard Book Number 978-0-88270-491-3

Scripture quotations marked KJV are from the *King James Version* of the Bible.

Scripture quotations marked NKJV are taken from the *New King James Version.* Copyright © 1979, 1980, 1982 by Thomas Nelson, Inc. Used by permission. All rights reserved.

Scripture quotations marked NASB are taken from the *New American Standard Bible.* Copyright © 1960, 1962, 1963, 1968, 1971, 1972, 1973, 1975, 1977, 1995 by The Lockman Foundation. Used by permission.

Scripture quotations marked NIV are taken from the *Holy Bible, New International Version®.* NIV®. Copyright © 1973, 1978, 1984 by International Bible Society. Used by permission of Zondervan. All rights reserved.

Cover design by Elizabeth Nason

G218.316.N.m1004.35260

Contents

Foreword

I don't like fishing because it's boring. I prefer catching—and it was the thought of catching fish that excited me about spending an entire day fishing with newfound friends on a beautiful lake in Oregon. We *did* catch fish (I pulled in three), but the size and total amount didn't exactly sink the boat. Still, because of the great fellowship during those long hours of mostly waiting, I wasn't bored.

One of the fellows on the boat was Marshall Alexander, and after hearing his incredible story I insisted he write a book. Many people have been as close to death as Marshall and they have also lived to tell the story, but I believed this one was different. It is different because of what happened leading up to the crash. It is different because of his amazing attitude, and more importantly, the reason for that attitude. I would love to tell you what happened, but I will leave that up to him—in the hope that this book will be more than just another life-and-death drama.

Ray Comfort
Founder/President/CEO
Living Waters Publications

Preface

I was reading and praying a little while ago and had some thoughts about what this book did and did not say. In many ways it is incomplete because it does not tell all the stories of my life and it contains large blank spots. It does not answer every question someone might ask while trying to read between the lines. I don't want to leave the impression I am perfect, have never sinned, have no failings, or that I do everything right.

The book you have before you is about an amazing miracle God demonstrated in my life a few years ago on a cold, dark mountainside in the Pacific Northwest. The story is told along with some anecdotes and stories about my life before and after that miracle night.

I am not a great saint of God, a nationally known personality with a large following, or a man without faults and challenges. The book is not a tell-all story of my failings or my accomplishments. It is simply a story about how the love of God endures throughout one man's life and proves that God's Word can be trusted.

My story indicates that life is a marathon with the goal of running well in God's eyes and finishing the race. I took some wrong turns during the race, but managed to find my way back on course. I have had to run the race through obstacles and storms that have made me want to quit at times, but by the grace of God and through His strength I have continued. I have found the joy of the Lord while running and overcoming the obstacles. The book reveals that I am still running the race; it is not over until it is over.

I am simply an ordinary guy who loves his heavenly Father, and now knows more than ever after that dark night of March 16, 2007, that my heavenly Father loves me. You, too, could be that same ordinary guy or gal. I hope this story encourages you and forces you to your knees to realize and accept that the same God I serve can also be your everlasting joy.

Marshall J. Alexander
Klamath Falls, Oregon

Chapter 1

Preparing to Die

Beloved, think it not strange concerning the fiery trial which is to try you, as though some strange thing happened unto you: But rejoice, inasmuch as ye are partakers of Christ's sufferings; that, when his glory shall be revealed, ye may be glad also with exceeding joy. (1 Peter 4:12-13, kjv)

March 2007

I was about to die.

The plane was out of gas. I was only fifty feet above a snowcapped mountain, skimming the treetops in the blackness of a moonless night. If I hit a tree, I would more than likely end up like most pilots in a similar situation: impaled by a branch as it smashed through the cockpit. If I plowed into the mountain, either I would die instantly from the massive impact, or I would break every bone in my body and die a slow death. Either way, the result would be death. I pulled two pillows from behind me and arranged them to lessen the impact, took off my glasses, and waited.

1

Mount Rainier 1978

This was not the first time I had been on a mountain near death's door. The first incident happened when I climbed Mount Rainier in Washington State many years ago. I was climbing with four others—two experienced climbers and two novices: two men and two women. That day in early July started out with sun and some broken clouds. For this climb, we were going to take the easy route up to Camp Muir at 10,000 feet for base camp, and take the Cowlitz/Ingraham Glacier to the summit the following day. By early afternoon the weather had deteriorated from sun to partial clouds, then snow, fog, and finally we were enveloped in a whiteout. We roped ourselves together to ensure none of us got lost in the gale. Climbing with a ninety-five-pound pack full of climbing gear is hard, but when you add to that the mental obstacle of not being able to see five feet in front of you and the vertigo from the snow and fog, you might as well be carrying double the weight. The sea of whiteness surrounding us gave me a very eerie feeling.

Without warning, one of the climbers in our party belly-flopped into the snow. She indicated she couldn't go on. The moment turned tense, and I yelled through the sound of the wind and the whirling snow, "We have to keep going! We're too exposed here and there's no place to set up the tents." I knew from experience that digging in here would take as much energy as climbing on, so somehow we had to keep moving.

I thought the woman who fell was an experienced climber, yet now it was clear that she didn't know her limits. She had pushed herself as far as she could; for her, there was no going on. We couldn't carry her to the summit—the

2

human body is just too awkward a package to bear while climbing a snow-covered mountain—yet turning back was not a viable choice. Behind their snow goggles, I could see tension—and fear—growing on the team members' faces.

Stopping for a rest was not an option. Again, I yelled through the fog, "We have to keep going! We'll die of exposure if we stop here!"

The woman climber finally mustered the determination to get up and keep climbing. She dug deep and found a reserve of energy and the will to keep going. Relief washed over the rest of us.

We climbed for another hour, gaining some elevation. My altimeter indicated about 8,500 feet—only 1,500 more to go. I was getting tired and the wet snow made everything heavy and hindered our progress. Once again I heard, "I can't go on! I just can't!"

I told the group to rest while I scouted the area to see if there was a suitable spot to set up camp. We needed something that wasn't at a forty-five- to sixty-five-degree slope and that had a ridge or rock outcropping to block the wind. As the wind and snow steadily picked up, my chances of finding a suitable spot decreased.

I took off my backpack—which is always risky—to make it easier to scout the area. Were I to get separated from the group in this whiteout, I wouldn't have any shelter or supplies with which to survive the elements. As the leader, I was responsible for four other lives. Alone and without supplies, I climbed ahead. After a fruitless search for a suitable area to set up camp, I turned back, hoping I'd find my backpack and my team. I made it back to the others safely, but was discouraged to discover that the other four climbers were growing cold from having stopped, and they didn't want to go any farther.

I was horrified when one of the climbers said in a weak, shaky voice, "I can't go on. Just leave me here to die."

Suddenly, my fun, friendly, weekend mountain climb had turned deadly serious. I took the pack from the woman having the most trouble and attached it to mine, bringing my load to around 160 pounds. At the time, I only weighed 160 pounds. Not exactly built like Mr. Universe, I had to rely on the strength of my iron will to keep putting one foot in front of the other without collapsing under the weight. Slowly, we climbed another 1,000 feet in elevation, stopping only when we found a flat place to dig in for the night.

A few of us began to quickly dig out a pad for the two tents. Our progress was going well, but I began to notice the uncontrolled shivering and slurred speech of two members of the group—early signs of hypothermia. We had to get the tents up soon and get everyone out of this cold, now life-threatening weather.

Fighting the cold, numbing wind, the tents were finally up and we quickly got the sleeping bags out. Initially, we all crowded into one tent to help warm each other. We helped the two hypothermic members exchange their cold, wet clothes for dry, warmer clothes and put them in their sleeping bags. I asked the two remaining climbers to help warm them up by lying next to them with their bags covering all four of them. While they were attempting to warm each other up and defeat the hypothermia, I went to the other tent to warm up hot water for hot chocolate and a warm dinner. Fortunately, the Svea 123 stove started up quickly and began producing effective heat with its distinctive blowtorch sound. Within minutes, we got through the anxious moments and regained our composure while sipping hot chocolate.

We all survived the night, and three of the five in the group made the summit the next day. The other two stayed with the tents until our descent. I couldn't have known it then, but the God-given determination it took to save my friend from dying on the mountain would one day save my own life when I crashed my plane in the lonely winter wilderness of the Cascade Mountains.

June 2007

It was just three months after the crash, mid-June 2007, before my plane was recovered with most of my personal belongings. My Palm Pilot, camera, and laptop spent the winter up in the mountains. All three items were just sitting out on the mountainside when the recovery crew arrived at the crash site. I had driven up to the staging area near the crash site to join a crew with the helicopter that was prepared to pull the airplane off the mountain. It had been determined that the only way to recover the airplane was to have a helicopter lift it out while attached to a cable.

The plane practically broke in half when it was being lifted, and many of my belongings fell onto the ground. I was hopeful I would be able to recover all of my belongings— and I recovered nearly all of them; the rest I came back for later in August.

Everything was wet and moldy and it looked like mice, or some hungry critter, had eaten through part of the briefcase.

5

Even though almost everything was in terrible shape, I did not care; I was thrilled to have found something. Hours later, while the crew began to disassemble my airplane to haul it off the mountain, I placed everything on the tailgate of my truck, piece by piece, to dry out in the sun for the four or five hours I worked on the plane. I turned on my Dell computer, and it started right up—even the battery still worked! In fact, I still use that same laptop today. I thought about sending my story to Dell to see if they might want to give me a new computer, but I never have.

However, as I continued to inspect all the items that I recovered, it was evident that my Nikon camera was broken. I mailed the camera and my story to Nikon—the same story that I had written for the insurance agency—and explained:

> Dear Sirs:
>   I crashed my airplane and broke this camera in the crash. I don't know if you are able to fix it, but here is a copy of the story of the plane crash. Thank you for your time and consideration.
>
> Sincerely,
> Marshall Alexander

Nikon read the story and were generous enough to fix my camera for free. After the experience with Nikon, my friends still encourage me to send my story to Dell, and maybe, with God's help, I will work up the nerve to do it.

Inside my critter-chewed-on briefcase was *The Basic Training Course* manual from Kirk Cameron and Ray

Comfort's ministry. It was still intact, along with my *Evidence Bible*, and a bunch of gospel tracts from Living Waters Publications. My first thought was, *Wouldn't it have been amazing if a hunter or hiker had stumbled upon all my Christian literature just lying there in the snow, read it, repented, and received Christ?*

But maybe I should go back a bit ...

Love of Flying

I don't remember where my love for flying came from—I was never in an airplane until I signed up for the Air Force ROTC (Reserve Officers' Training Corps) at the University of Washington. I do, however, remember the space race of the early 1960s. Its coverage dominated newspaper headlines, magazine covers, and the *Weekly Reader* at school. The color photos on the cover of *Life* magazine were mind-boggling. Lying in bed as a boy, I would often dream of soaring with the eagles as a means of escape from the nightmares of life. Many times, dressed in my pint-sized Superman costume, I would attempt to fly. Oh, the flights went well enough—it was the landings that needed work. But more on my "solo" flight career later.

I was rather sheltered from the things of the world. My family never went on real vacations, so our life was pretty much confined to the local neighborhood. If we could walk or ride our bikes there, it was part of our life; if we had to drive there, we didn't know it existed. I lived in southern California for nine years while growing up, but never saw Disneyland or the many other attractions the area had to offer. The only outing I went on was with my Cub Scout troop to a Los Angeles Angels baseball game.

My first real trip was also the first time I ever set foot on an airplane. It was an event that helped mold the rest of my life. I started my higher education at the University of Washington in Seattle. Within a few weeks, I'd signed up for the ROTC and boarded my first airplane—a huge prop-powered transport—that flew us to a ROTC outing. The seats were very uncomfortable sling-types, like you see on old jump planes in the movies. It seems like such a long time ago, yet I remember it as though I were still that naïve, provincial college boy.

We took off out of Seattle and headed to Vandenberg Air Force Base in California for a tour of the missile silos. I was berthed in the officers' quarters with my own room. I felt mature and important at eighteen years of age, wearing my blue officer's uniform and having a much older airman salute me. It was quite a contrast to wearing the same uniform on the U of W's campus twice a week during the Vietnam anti-war protests and Students for a Democratic Society demonstrations. College campuses during those years were not the most welcoming venues for a military presence, as we were seen as future warmongers. All of my uncles had served in World War II or Korea, so despite the difficulties on campus, I was proud to be in the military. Besides, it was my means to an end: becoming a pilot. Unfortunately, things did not turn out well for my flying career in the Air Force. The results of my Air Force eye exam when I was eighteen forever closed the door to that dream. Instead, I became a banker, and my goal of becoming a pilot was put on hold.

My first professional job out of college was working for a regional bank in Sunnyside, Washington. One of the bank's potential clients was a Bible bookstore in town. I first began calling on the store and its owner, Wayne Ginther, as part of my job, but soon the business relationship developed into a friendship. Through our friendship Wayne introduced me to mountain climbing, and to other Christians who enjoyed backpacking and mountain climbing. I began attending his church regularly. My first flight instructor was the co-pastor at the church. He encouraged me in many ways and taught me to rise above all of the cares of the world, and to understand that people may fail you, but God never will. He is the same yesterday, today, and forever. Taking lessons from my pastor was great, but eventually I moved from Sunnyside, Washington, to Joseph, Oregon, to begin work at another bank, and had to find a new instructor. The flight instructor I found was young and I did not know at the time, but I was his first student to get a pilot's license. Now I understand why he was so nervous when he sent me out on my *first* solo flight. Within a year of starting lessons, I had my private pilot's license.

March 2007, the story begins …

Why the Flight?

After a nice warm day of yardwork, pruning trees and raking leaves, I received a phone call from my brother-in-law in Springfield, Oregon, around 7:00 P.M. He said that my sister Debby had suffered a heart attack and was in the hospital. She was doing okay but would need to stay in the hospital a few more days. The next day, their two adult children would be flying home from Boise and Los Angeles to be with them. (Ironically, it turned out Debby was fine and actually came to see me a few days after the crash.)

9

I told my brother-in-law I could fly over that night and be with them over the weekend if he could pick me up at the Eugene Airport. After I checked the weather, I would call him to let him know if I was coming for sure.

I was looking forward to getting away from home for a bit; it would be a break from the emotional issues we had been experiencing with two of our children. My wife consented, yet I sensed she had reservations. Women are funny that way; they seem to have built-in radar that we men ought to recognize better. Being a typical guy, I ignored this subtle warning sign, took a shower, and then began mentally planning my preflight for the trip.

The weather forecast I saw on the Internet was clear: no clouds, no precipitation, and no wind throughout the route. It looked good through Sunday.

I called my brother-in-law and told him I would be flying over and asked him to meet me around 10:30 P.M. at Flight Craft in Eugene, Oregon. My plane definitely needed fuel, so I drove out to the airport in my old pickup with its 100-gallon extra fuel tank filled with aviation fuel. I parked my truck in front of the hangar, as usual, in order to refuel the plane, and then walked into the hangar to prepare for the flight.

I went through my normal airplane preflight walk-around and checklist:

- Fuel? Check. I've got the truck and I'll get to that in a minute.
- Oil level okay? Check.
- Alternator belt good? Check.
- Tires good? Check.

- Strobes working? Check.
- Landing light on? Check.

My sister's house would be full and every bed taken, leaving me to sleep on the floor. Part of my usual wintertime emergency gear includes a sleeping bag and pad, so I was set as far as sleeping arrangements go. Taking the sleeping bag and pad, I spotted two pillows. They'd take up room I really didn't have to spare, but I grabbed them anyway. Another check to make sure I had all the equipment I might need:

- Expensive satellite phone I've never used? Check.
- Camera? Check.
- Portable oxygen with two oxysaver cannulas attached? Check.
- Flashlight? Check.
- Handheld transceiver? Check.
- Mag light with red lens? Check.
- Current sectionals? Check.
- Water and snacks? Check.
- Sleeping bag, pad, and pillows? Check.

I turned the oxygen tank on and adjusted the flow for 12,500 feet. I stuffed the sleeping bag and extra equipment into the aft storage, and was about to stuff the two pillows in, but decided to put them on the backseat instead.

Once again, I mentally went through my checklist as I looked through the plane. Everything was in order; I hadn't forgotten a thing.

I was ready for takeoff.

All I had to do now was move my fuel truck out of the way, pull the plane out, lock the hangar, and I would finally be on my way. Thoughts of my sister were continually going through my mind. Was she still stable? Would she be okay until I got there? She was so young to have had a heart attack. Why now? Now's not a good time. It's never a good time for things like this to happen. My wife, Judy, really needed my help with the kids back at home and this wasn't a convenient time to be leaving.

Okay, Marshall. Remember, God's in control and "all things work together for good to those who love God," I reminded myself.

The roar of the airplane's engine starting up snapped me back to full awareness. I listened to the ATIS to prepare for taxi and takeoff. I taxied to runway 14, with a right downwind departure, proceeded with the normal before-take-off ramp check, the extra night flight check, set the cabin and panel lights, preset frequencies, and double-checked everything while waiting for the oil and engine temperatures to come up to normal ranges. Thorough preparation, checking, and double-checking is key to air safety.

Filing a flight plan is recommended, as its purpose is to help air traffic controllers and rescue personnel know where to look if there is a problem and they need to look for a downed aircraft. I didn't feel it was necessary to file a flight plan since I was flying direct, Klamath Falls to Eugene—a short hour-and-twenty-minute flight. I had talked to my wife and let her know I would take off around 9:00 P.M. and that my brother-in-law would be waiting for me at Flight Craft at 10:30 P.M. If anything were to happen, my family would know my flight path. I would monitor Klamath

Tower, Cascade Approach, and Eugene Tower during the flight.

Within minutes, I took off without incident and was soon proceeding directly to Eugene, Oregon, at a climb of seven hundred feet per minute, to a cruising altitude of 12,500 feet.

It was a clear, moonless night. The sky and ground were both very dark, but the air was cool and smooth. Between Klamath Falls and Eugene there are no towns and few houses or buildings—just the rugged Cascade Mountains. I was breathing oxygen from my portable tank and was settled in, enjoying the dark, yet smooth flight. Evening flights in the winter are the best, if you have no weather concerns. The air is always smooth, requiring few corrections on the yoke to keep on course. Lights on the ground sparkle and look magnificent. Anyone who has flown in a commercial airliner at night has felt that magical sensation when looking at city lights from the air as they come in for a landing. Small private planes do not fly that high, so city lights at night always give a feeling of enchantment.

CHAPTER 2

The Emergency

AND WE KNOW THAT IN ALL THINGS GOD WORKS FOR THE
GOOD OF THOSE WHO LOVE HIM, WHO HAVE BEEN CALLED
ACCORDING TO HIS PURPOSE. (ROMANS 8:28, NIV)

The night was beautiful and the weather was perfect for flying. The stars were shining brightly against the dark sky, seeming to light my way. I had just begun to see the lights of Eugene on the horizon and I glanced down at my GPS. Only forty-two kilometers to Eugene. *Piece of cake,* I thought to myself.

Monitoring the Eugene Tower frequency, I was preparing to switch to approach to get flight following into Eugene when I had a horrifying realization: I had been at the airport, doing my preflight checklist … *"Fuel? Check— I'll get to that in a minute …"* I hadn't fueled up! My truck had been right there, and I hadn't fueled up!

Frantic, I grabbed my flashlight and pointed it toward the ceiling. I shined it on the right fuel gauge. Empty. I flicked to the left fuel gage. Empty. Both were pegged in the

15

red. I shook my wings, hoping to see movement on the fuel gauges. Nothing. My heart dropped. I had an immediate sinking, nauseating feeling: *I'm dead.*

Try not to panic, Marshall. You know what to do. My thoughts were nominally comforting.

I switched my transponder to 7700, indicating to all local towers and radar that I had an emergency. I zoomed out on the GPS to see if there was a closer airport.

Yes! Toketee State Airstrip was closer, but it was behind me now. It was a small grass Forest Service strip, with no lights, surrounded by mountains, and would be covered in snow at this time of year. It calls for a skilled landing in the daylight in the middle of the summer, but tonight it was winter and pitch-black. I'd never attempted to land there, but my GPS didn't indicate any other possible landing sites. I began thinking, *This is it; I'm going home to be with Jesus tonight.*

I was comfortable with that thought, knowing my eternal destiny was secure. I had known for a long time I was going to Heaven when I died.

For a brief moment I thought about the weekly Bible studies I held in my home using the evangelism training course, *The Way of the Master*, developed by Kirk Cameron and Ray Comfort. Assessing my situation, I was thankful I'd been able to share the gospel with my friends, family, and others, as I was sure I wouldn't survive to share it again. I recalled telling people, "Now is the time to repent of your sins and trust Jesus with your life, because you don't know when you are going to die." I recognized the irony in those words, as I *did* know when I was going to die: within the hour.

I put in a call to Eugene Tower and, in as calm a voice as I could muster, declared an emergency. While thinking to myself, *Stay in control, don't panic,* I spoke to Eugene Tower:

"This is Cessna November 6-4-6-2-Alpha. I am on a VFR flight, Klamath direct to Eugene. I'm cruising at twelve thousand five hundred, forty-two kilometers out, and will be out of fuel shortly. I'm anticipating I'll crash in the mountains. Please tell my wife I love her, and I'll see her in Heaven. Her phone number is ---/---/----."

I quickly repeated the message, as the knot in my stomach tightened. My hope was that they would receive my message, call my wife immediately, and let her know that her husband had just crashed. I waited for a response from Eugene Tower. I did not get the normal immediate response, which made me even more anxious. Hearing nothing, I checked my radio frequency settings. They seemed to be correct. Maybe I didn't hit the push-to-talk switch while trying to broadcast. I was wasting precious time. I started over. "This is Skylane 6-4-6-2-Alpha, I'm having an emergency. Looks like I'm going to be running out of fuel here ..."

About this time, the engine quit. Everything felt surreal, almost like I was dreaming. I told the Eugene Tower I was turning back southeast in an attempt to land at the Forest Service grass strip at Toketee. I knew it was probably under deep snow, but down the middle of the draw it would be clear of trees and rocks. If only I could make it there. I asked

Eugene if they had any suggestions or vectors to the nearest runway, and if they had any advice. The only response I got from the tower was, "Squawk 7700, remain this frequency."

This was a first for me. I had never adjusted a transponder to the emergency squawk of 7700 before. Dialing a transponder to 7700 is used for emergencies only. Pilots normally read the flight manuals and periodically review emergency procedures as part of keeping up-to-date and being a good pilot, so it is something almost every pilot knows. But to actually see "7700" dialed up on your airplane transponder—that is a scary moment. Then, to hear the tower tell you "Squawk 7700," means they know you are involved in a real emergency. Everyone listening in on the tower frequency knows there is a frantic pilot flying out in the eerie, black night over the rugged Cascades who is trying to stay calm while knowing that, in all probability, only bad things are going to happen within a matter of minutes.

Transcript of the Emergency Crash Call:

Marshall:

"Eugene Tower, this is Skyline 6462-Alpha, I'm declaring an emergency. Looks like I'm going to be running out of fuel here ... I have ..."

Eugene Tower:

"Just heard from a Cessna. It looks like he is going to run out of fuel."

Marshall:

"I'm out of fuel, so I'm going to be crashing. Tell my wife I love her, if you can get this. I have no idea where I am. I'm in the mountains ... Um ... Oh, well ..."

Eugene Tower:

"November 6462-Alpha, Cascade approach or Eugene Tower Squawk 7700. If you have a transponder squawk 7700."

(Woman): "Tom, he's doing it. Tom, it looks like he's maybe sixty miles north of Medford, probably sixty miles or closer. Looks like he is closer to Roseburg. I'll see if I can get a better visual."

(Man): "Okay, he says he's already out of fuel. He's going down."

Marshall:

"I have no idea where I'm going from here."

Eugene Tower:

"6462-Alpha, looks like they've got your transponder. You're flying about sixty miles north of the Medford airport. Do you copy?"

Marshall:

"Affirmative."

Eugene Tower:

"Okay, we're trying to get a better location. So you're out of fuel at this time?"

Marshall:

"Right. I'm heading toward ... probably ... Medford. I'm just in the lights. I'm heading toward the light. I'm assuming the lights are Medford. I'm on a heading of 1-8-4."

Eugene Tower:

"Okay, and say your altitude for 6462-Alpha."

Marshall:

"Currently 9300 and descending. I'm at maximum glide, so I'm hoping to get down there somewhere."

Eugene Tower:

"Okay, 6462-Alpha; roger. Remain on this frequency, please."

(Woman): "At Medford showing a 7700 squawk …"

(Man): "Are you ready?"

(Woman): "Yeah. Go ahead Center …"

(Man): "He said he is on a 184 degrees heading east, he's at 9.3. He's at maximum glide. He's just kinda hoping he makes it."

(Woman): "Okay, let me see if I can talk to the Center and see if I can get him clearance for an emergency airport."

(Man): "Is he out of fuel?"

(Woman): "Yes. He's at 180 heading … He's at glide ratio, and he's out of fuel. Do you have any close airports?"

Marshall:

"If you determine my location, could you indicate where I might hit or land, so I could slow it down, slow it down really slow?"

Eugene Tower:

"6462-Alpha, we're talking with Center right now. We're trying to locate an emergency airport in your area there, if we can. Try to find you someplace that you can touch down."

Marshall:

"I know I'm going to hit down soon; I'm at 8300 now."

Eugene Tower:

(Woman): "Three point nine miles. Three point nine miles north of his position is Toketee airport."

(Man): "What is it?"

(Woman): "Toketee airport, it's what Center says."

(Man): "Three point nine miles north? Is it lit? No, it is not lit, is it?"

(Woman): "It's not."

Marshall:

"I know I just passed Toketee. It is just a grass strip."

Eugene Tower:

"6462-Alpha, Center advises that 3.9 nautical miles north of your position is a small airport called Toketee. I'm trying to pull up some paperwork on it, and find out where it's at."

(noise)

Eugene Tower:

"6462-Alpha, did you copy that?"

(Woman): "Do you have any information on ..."

(Man): "I'm trying to look it up."

(Man): "I don't have anything else. It's about eleven. Touchdown 5300 ft. We're about five miles from location."

(Woman): "Five miles. Six miles north."

(Man): "He's going to need to reverse if he wants to get there."

(Woman): "Okay, I'll advise."

(Man): "Okay, I copy all that. I'm going to try to get a hold of him, switch him to a Medford frequency."

(Woman): "He's nowhere near Medford, Tom."

(Man): "Okay."

(Woman): "If anything, he should be talking to …"

(Man): "Okay, I'm going to try to switch him over there if I can. Hey 6462-Alpha, do you still copy? November 6462-Alpha, if you copy Eugene Tower, contact 1-2-1 decimal 4."

(Woman): "What is your position for emergency services for him? Is there anything like that? Who should I be calling for 911?"

(Man): "We're going to have to find someone else for that. We have no way of …"

(Woman): "Okay, well it looks like the supervisor's out right now, so if you have a supervisor to initiate those calls, I will make the handoff to you, as far as that goes."

(Man): "Yeah. Okay, Tom, we lost radar on him, so I don't know if he's reversed course or not."

(Woman): "Yeah, we lost radar as well."

(Man): "I'm trying to switch frequencies, but I don't think he can hear me anymore. He was calling Eugene Tower."

(Woman): "Yeah, he was calling Eugene Tower, but they've lost radio communications now, also."

(Man): "November 6462-Alpha, if you hear Eugene Tower, contact Seattle Center 1-2-1 decimal 4."

Marshall's Recollection Continues

As I turned left, to the south, I saw Roseburg. It didn't look that far off. The city lights were bright and appeared pretty close. I attempted to dial up Roseburg on the GPS to see how far it really was. I maintained an approximate south heading, maintaining maximum glide at eighty miles per hour while trying to see if I could make Roseburg. I did not finish my assessment because, on my next glance at Roseburg, I saw fewer and fewer lights—which meant the terrain was blocking them from my sight. Going in that direction would be impossible. I turned more southeast, hoping to reach the small, dark, snowed-in landing strip at Toketee.

I continued transmitting in the blind to Eugene Tower, with no response. I indicated my elevation, direction, and intent. At this point I figured I was too low for Medford Tower to reach me, but I kept transmitting anyway. Airplane radios basically work by line-of-sight, which normally works very well because airplanes are high in the air, so obstructions—like mountains—are not a factor. Additionally, knowing that mountains can inhibit airplane transmissions, there are repeaters on mountaintops and in remote areas that pick up radio signals and retransmit them. However, you have to be tuned to the correct frequency, and the correct frequencies are for flight centers and flight services, not local towers. As I was not asked to switch to

Seattle Center at 121.4 until after I was too low, I didn't hear Medford Tower's request.

I transmitted: "Eight thousand five hundred feet, gliding steadily downward."

"Seven thousand feet. Terrain is coming up on the horizon and impact with terrain will happen shortly."

My chances were slim, but I had to give it everything I had. Combating my mounting fear, I kicked my iron will into gear, focused hard to keep the airplane under control for as long as I could, and waited for the sound of a human voice over the radio. It never came.

Below me were dark shadows of varying shades I assumed were the ground and surrounding terrain. The truth was I had no idea what was in front of me or below me. The one thing I was certain of was that this time, my iron will wasn't enough; I wasn't going to make it to Toketee.

I stopped looking at the GPS and tried to see outside the airplane. The sky and horizon were so dark it was hard to distinguish between them. I decided the dark stuff was earth, with granite cliffs and big trees, and the sort-of-dark stuff was the night sky.

I told God I would be with Him in a couple of more minutes. My flight—and my life—were almost over.

CHAPTER 3

Early Life and First Birth

FOR THOSE GOD FOREKNEW HE ALSO PREDESTINED TO BE
CONFORMED TO THE LIKENESS OF HIS SON, THAT HE MIGHT
BE THE FIRSTBORN AMONG MANY BROTHERS. AND THOSE
HE PREDESTINED, HE ALSO CALLED; THOSE HE CALLED, HE
ALSO JUSTIFIED; THOSE HE JUSTIFIED, HE ALSO GLORIFIED.
(ROMANS 8:29-30, NIV)

Summer 2009

My oldest sister, Starlene, and I were sitting in Mom's hospital room thinking about the once caring, nurturing, and energetic woman who now seemed so frail, confused, and vulnerable. We shared the thought that we could lose both our mom and dad within the span of a year.

Mom had been fighting leukemia for years, and had recently had her spleen removed as part of the ongoing battle. She had so many ups and downs with her health that we weren't sure she would have the strength to keep up the fight. We were comforted in knowing Mom's life was in God's hands, and that she was ready to go home to Him when He called her name.

Dad had been diagnosed with lung cancer over a year before, and had been given three to four months to live. As Starlene and I sat in Mom's hospital room that day, it was fifteen months after that diagnosis, and Dad was closer than ever to realizing his destiny was in God's hands.

While Starlene and I talked about the possibility of losing both Mom and Dad within the near future, our conversation became nostalgic. After a few "remember whens?" I realized that somehow the story of how our parents had met had escaped my attention. As Starlene unfolded their romantic tale for me, I looked at Mom, a slight, shriveled old woman, lying helpless in her hospital bed. I looked away, back into the past, and tried to see Mom as she must have looked years ago, as a vibrant young girl.

The Post-War 1940s

My parents' generation of the Alexanders all started at a little diner-car-turned-restaurant up north in Moses Lake, Washington. Starlene told me how Mom worked at that restaurant in the summers of 1947 and 1948, earning money to attend Multnomah Bible School in Portland, Oregon. Picturing Mom as a girl in a waitress uniform made me smile. Starlene told me how a handsome young man came in for supper one evening and struck up a conversation with "that cute little waitress." Yes, Mom must have looked awfully cute, running around with hot plates of food and pots of coffee. That young man later wrote the little waitress a love song:

26

Oh, Oh, Oh, I love you sooooo,
Oh, Oh, I love you soooooo.
In a little diner, in a little town up north ...

So much love and promise. So much potential. And not a glimpse of the craziness that would later shake the Alexander family like chaotic turbulence shakes a small plane.

Now, fifty-plus years later, my oldest sister, Starlene, and her husband live in that same town where it all began, Moses Lake, Washington. A few years ago, Starlene called me and told me about an experience she had that she attributed to the leading of the Holy Spirit. She was driving through town and noticed the little diner. She soon found herself standing in front of the diner-car-turned-restaurant at about 10:00 P.M.—the same place that Mom and Dad met. Except for the streetlights, she was surrounded by darkness. She cried out to God to have mercy on her parents and to work everything out for His glory and our family's good.

Bill and Stella

My mother believed she was called to the mission field, and since childhood, my father had felt called to preach. When we were children, he would tell us of the times he would open his garage door and invite his classmates to come and hear him preach there, while enduring the ridicule of his mother and brothers.

Yet my maternal grandmother would not consent to their marriage unless Stella, my mother, agreed to continue her plan to attend Bible college. She also insisted that Bill, my dad, attend the college, should he be accepted. Within

27

a few short months, the college accepted his application. Stella and Bill got married and had attended the college for about thirty days when Bill voiced his opinions not only of the nation's politics and policies, but of the church's as well. He had just returned from a Pacific tour with the US Navy during World War II and was a gung-ho patriot and Christian, so he freely expressed his concerns while at college. He was puzzled by the response—the Bible college insisted he abide by the American government's separation of church and state—and that he stop zealously mixing the two. Always a great idealist, he did neither, and was asked to leave the college on the grounds that he was disrupting the school's goals of teaching the gospel message.

Having entered college with great idealism and the grand expectations he had of living among "real Christians," young Bill was vulnerable to the reality of the human condition. Looking back I can see that my dad was a false convert—he had come to Christ for the wrong reasons. He tried to cling to the message that "God loves you and has a wonderful plan for your life," without realizing that the wonderful plan is often strewn with trials, temptations, and adversities. Dad was looking for God to make him happy, solve all of his problems, and rescue him from the hassles of this life. The prosperity gospel was mixed with the expectation that God was going to make him a millionaire, if he only believed enough. Greatly disillusioned and disappointed by the hypocrisy they'd met, the newlyweds left Bible school.

They moved to Brewster, Washington, to be near my dad's relatives and to find work. Despite his early fire for Christ, time proved my father fit the description of the seed sown on the rocky soil—the soil where the seed bursts up, but soon withers because of the heat, or the cares of this world.

Idealistic, creative, and a born instructor, my dad never lost his love of talking about the purpose of life—from his point of view. His changing worldview rose to great heights, only to crash against the shores of reality. The regularity with which this occurred created tidal waves in our family that washed over us all. As the swells of life continued, we were all pushed further and further from the truths of God's Word, into the ocean of a man-made theology.

The Family

Within a year of leaving the Bible college, Mom and Dad's first child, Starlene, was born in Brewster, Washington. As the need to support a wife and child grew beyond what Dad could earn in rural Brewster, the Alexander family moved back to the big city of Portland, Oregon. Dad found employment and, during the celebration of that success, I was conceived. Nine months later, I was born at the Portland Sanitarium in Portland, Oregon. Fifteen months after I was born, my second sibling, Debby, arrived. The Alexander family now had five members, and my dad needed more income. He decided it was time to leave Portland and move to the land of milk and honey—southern California.

Two of my dad's God-given gifts were his abilities to draw and to put his thoughts and ideas on paper. To capitalize on these skills, he packed up his family and moved to southern California to be a tool designer/draftsman in the booming aeronautical industry.

We attended church fairly regularly until I was about six years old, but during this time, Dad struggled with bitterness. His falsely perceived promise of God's blessings, along with the hypocrisy he saw in churchgoers, seemed to create a mind-set and a lie he would hold on to for the next fifty years. It was soon apparent that Dad was rocky soil. Over time, our father's desperate attempts to stay positive while groaning under the weight of bitterness and disillusionment took its toll, and he lost his first love for Jesus. God's Word and its truths became mere tools to validate a new theology based on human reasoning.

The Alexander family increased again with our baby sister Danette. At the time, Starlene was five, I was four, and Debby was two.

Mental Illness

While we were growing up, Mom suffered frightening episodes of mental illness. Today some understand it as a hereditary chemical imbalance passed on through the family line, but back then Mom's tumultuous periods were labeled as nervous breakdowns, schizophrenic attacks, satanic attacks, demon possession, and just plain escapism. The mood swings were so great she sometimes needed hospitalization, leaving us without our mother for sometimes weeks and months while she recovered. Mom would not be properly diagnosed until she was in her thirties, and then the correct medication would keep her mood swings near normal.

To my recollection, we would have a few years— sometimes up to four years—of relative calm before Mom's illness resulted in another life-changing disruption. During our times of relative calm, we experienced the childlike faith of our mother. The simple acts of my mother's love demonstrated that the God she served was a God of love and worthy of worship, to be trusted in all things.

Family Times

Saturday nights were the nights we got out our best shoes to polish so that they were ready the next morning for Sunday school. After the shoes were polished, we traced the soles of the shoes on cardboard and set the cardboard cutout inside the shoes to cover the holes. This type of shoe "repair" was something everyone did, but I would rather have gone barefoot. If Mom weren't too busy, we would then have an evening story, oftentimes from some big, orange *Childcraft* book. They were not necessarily Christian stories, but usually had good morals and life lessons. Evening prayers were a priority, even when she was busy. The next morning, dressed in our finest handmade clothes, we would head off to church. These were the best of memories, and despite the tumultuous periods, the memories and lessons we learned during these times were the ones that shaped our young lives, moving us closer to the goal of being Christ like.

CHAPTER 4

1958-1961: My Conversion Story and Second Birth

BLESSED BE THE GOD AND FATHER OF OUR LORD JESUS CHRIST, WHO ACCORDING TO HIS GREAT MERCY HAS CAUSED US TO BE BORN AGAIN TO A LIVING HOPE THROUGH THE RESURRECTION OF JESUS CHRIST FROM THE DEAD.
(1 PETER 1:3, NASB)

These were busy years and perhaps the happiest for the Alexander family. Dad and Mother were the PTA presidents for our school. Mother continued her volunteer efforts as a Brownie and Cub Scout leader, attending church at times. Dad was working regularly on his many inventions, but his church attendance dwindled and then stopped.

Starlene and I were given permission to walk to and attend any or all of the services at a little Baptist church near our grade school. We loved our young pastor and his wife. Starlene and I would often show up as the only attendees for evening services, so the enterprising young couple, the Ekenbergs, would offer to let us choose our favorite Bible story. After the story, they'd call our parents to obtain permission to take us with them to another church for that evening. They also conducted the Good News Club on Thursdays, which all four of us children regularly attended. From the fruit of their service, Starlene and I both experienced the convicting and saving power of Jesus, and were baptized at a young age. During one of the missionary stories in the Good News Club, Starlene felt God tugging at her heart to surrender her life to whatever He would call her to do, and she felt called to be a missionary in South America. She was nine years old. Her salvation experience, baptism, and call to missions were to be the bedrock of her life in the turbulent years to come.

It was also during one of the Sunday school classes at the little Baptist church in Arlington, California, when I was seven years old, that I was convicted of my sin and understood the need for a Savior. The Sunday school lesson was a flannel graph story. Flannel graph was the exciting multimedia format for children's Sunday school in the late 1950s. I remember the story was about a king who needed to teach one of his knights a lesson about life and the code of knighthood. The king told the knight that he needed to carry out the king's exact instructions, under penalty of death. The knight was to take a large bag of feathers into the forest, empty it into the forest wind, and return immediately. I recall the many feathers the teacher started placing on the board. Each feather had a word or phrase written on it. "Lying," "stealing," "hating," "disobeying parents," "wanting things your friends have," and "cussing" were a few. Even at that young age, I knew those feathers described bad, bad things.

The Sunday school teacher continued the story. Early the next morning, the king ordered the knight to go back to the forest and retrieve every feather he had released in the wind. The king knew every feather and had recorded each one. If the knight failed to bring back every one of those feathers, his penalty would be death.

The knight knew that the king had asked an impossible task. He tried to explain that to the king, but the king would not listen. The knight proceeded to the forest, knowing he would fail and his fate would be death.

The Sunday school teacher explained that those feathers are like sins; once we sin, we cannot ever take it back. She pointed out that God is like the king; He knows and remembers every one of our sins. We are like the knight, she said. One day we will return to the King and be responsible for every one of those sins. Just like the knight, unable to find all of the feathers and present them to his king, we can never account for all of our sins. Like that knight, our penalty would be death and we would spend eternity in hell. Only through the sacrifice of Jesus on the Cross, could the penalty of our disobedience—the penalty of our sin—be paid.

I had been to church regularly for most of my seven years and had heard about and believed in the reality of Heaven and hell, but for some reason, this simple illustration convicted me to the core. I had sin in my life, my spiritual death was certain, and I would spend eternity in hell.

As was the custom after Sunday school, we all sat with our parents or other adults and listened to the preacher's message. He always gave an altar call—a chance to come forward, be prayed for, and publicly acknowledge oneself to be a sinner in need of forgiveness. Through God's grace, our sin was forgiven, and our standing before God was made right. We, then, could look forward to spending eternity in Heaven with Jesus.

On this morning, I had no idea what the preacher preached. I was waiting impatiently (although "impatience" was a sin on one of the feathers) to go forward and repent and receive Jesus Christ as my Savior. At the appropriate time, I went forward and asked God to forgive me, and declared Jesus as the Lord of my life.

The flannel graph illustration so impressed me that I began making my own story pieces and inviting kids home after school and on weekends to hear the stories and the gospel and to receive Jesus as their Savior. Much like my father had been as a child, I was compelled to tell others about Jesus. At age seven, I was pretty much a neighborhood evangelist—I couldn't hold it in. Even though at that age I had not read the entire Bible, I knew Jesus. He was my friend, Savior, and Lord.

A Bright Spot: Chalk Talks

Our life in southern California in the 1950s wasn't always dark; there were a few bright spots. Dad began sharing the gospel using Chalk Talks, which fit both his artistic ability and his knack for spinning a yarn. Chalk Talks are a form of lecture where the speaker shares a story while drawing a picture with chalk. There were three types of chalk used: color that could be seen in sunlight or under white lights; color that glowed in the dark or under a black light; and the most special, invisible chalk—imperceptible in sunlight or under white lights. The black light chalk glows very brightly without light, but under a black light it glows even brighter and more intensely. The invisible chalk is white chalk. It looks invisible against a white paper background, and then glows with the various bright colors under the black light.

The artist-lecturer drew with the invisible chalk before the presentation began. The drawing was of an object or person and would be used as a surprise ending. Typically, white light is used in the beginning of the presentation, and as the story nears its conclusion, the white light is slowly dimmed and finally turned off. Working as Dad's assistant, dimming the lights on cue was often my job. I would turn big, custom-built knobs that moved hefty rheostats in a large box. Several dozen wires came out of the box and went to the various strategically placed lights, each adjusted to illuminate the large black velvet backdrop surrounding the Chalk Talk presentation. I still remember watching and helping my dad build all of this in our garage, not knowing how or what it was all for until the first night of his presentation.

At the conclusion, all the lights were dimmed and the black lights took over. When the black light came on, the invisible became visible. There was always a hush from the audience, followed by sounds of awe. Angels were one of the great surprises in some of the stories, unseen in the picture until the black light was turned on. One of the most powerful pictures was Jesus' tomb with the stone rolled in front of it. What was not seen at first was the angel. When the white lights were turned off and the black light was turned on, the stone was gone, and there stood a beautiful angel.

The Potter was one of Dad's favorite presentations. Using the special lights, the audience was convinced that the potter's wheel was spinning before their eyes. In this particular story, Dad emphasized the need to trust in the Potter's hands, especially when it seemed life was out of control. The clay is a perfect illustration for this as it spins and spins on the wheel, totally at the mercy of the Potter's hands. Conversely, Dad illustrated the purpose of the Potter's graveyard—the place where broken vessels were tossed because they were no longer pliable in the Potter's hands.

The Chalk Talk was an incredible educational tool. My father mastered this format and traveled both to churches and to secular events around southern California, drawing, telling stories, and teaching.

The Storms

A lot of the dark times in my life revolved around my mother's mental illness. I was too young to remember much about my mother's first episodes. I mostly remember staying with relatives on different occasions, and that my grandmother came and lived with us for a while. However, as I grew older, it became evident that all was not well with my mom. We kids witnessed some very disturbing—even horrifying—events as a result of her behavior. When I was ten, Mom experienced two more major episodes. As a result of them, I missed most of the fifth grade and my sister

Debby and I were sent to live with our great-aunt until the start of my sixth grade year. I'm not sure where my other two sisters were. Eventually, Dad, along with my other two sisters, came to pick us up. We all moved to Brewster, Washington, to start over—without Mom.

I wasn't sure how to define normal life. I had begun to withdraw and went into survival mode. My dad was trying hard, but things were not working out. Dad was not working, and we were forced to accept welfare. Dad was a very good artist, painting landscapes, portraits, and other works of art with oil paints on canvas. He planned to go on a road show just before Christmas to sell his paintings. My sister Starlene, now twelve years old, was playing "mom" at the time. One evening, as she was cooking dinner for us, she realized she needed something from the store. She and Dad went to the store while Debby, Danette, and I sat on the floor and watched a show on the black-and-white television.

The next thing we knew, the guy who supplied us with heating oil opened the back door and yelled at us to get out of the house fast! I looked back and saw the house was on fire. By opening the back door, oxygen was added to the flames and they roared all the more violently. We didn't have a phone, so I ran across the street to a motel, called the fire department, and then ran back home. I went back in the house and pulled out a few items, including the TV set, but failed to get anything of much worth. The fire department still had not arrived, so I ran across the street again and called for help. The house was going up in flames fast, probably because old newspapers stuffed in the walls had been used for insulation. Newspaper worked well for insulation, but even better as fuel for a fire.

My dad and my sister soon came home, and we all watched as the house continued to burn. The fire department never arrived and all of our belongings were lost in the fire. The biggest loss was two years' worth of oil paintings—Dad's hope to get us out of poverty.

The fire happened just before Christmas, 1962. We were a financially poor lot to begin with and lost even more in the fire. I don't recall having much in the way of clothes, toys, or anything else until after the fire. The community came to our family's aid, and with the Christmas spirit, gave us many essentials, and more. I personally benefited greatly, as I ended up with more nice new things—clothes, toys, and more—than I ever had before the fire. In fact, nearly fifty years later, I still have the handmade heavy quilt blanket that was given to me personally. Somehow, that handmade quilt has always followed me around.

With the need to start over again, we moved to nearby Bridgeport, Washington. I still believed Jesus was my Lord and Savior, but I was beginning to question and doubt He cared for children—at least the Alexander children. I don't know how or what my sisters were feeling at this time, but I was feeling abandoned, helpless, and hopeless. I tried to read my King James Bible and see if God's Word had the answers, but the language was difficult, my Christian maturity at age eleven was weak, and my faith was waning. At this point, I began to look around to see whom I admired and wanted to emulate and be like when I grew up. I decided I did not want to be like my parents or relatives and I saw no one in my life who gave me hope or guidance.

I started searching for answers, but never returned to the Bible. Instead, I prayed constantly for God to lead and guide me and get me out of the mess that was my life. My greatest escape was the school library. I began reading books, especially autobiographies and biographies of noted personalities. One book in particular changed my life.

It was the early 1960s and the space race was on. I was already interested in flying, astronomy, and space travel, so I read a biography of Charles Lindbergh. The aviator's life and exploits fascinated me. However, Lindbergh's life story and accomplishments were not what changed me; it was a simple statement he made in the book that had a great impact on me. As I recall, Lindbergh's statement went something like this:

> I had a very traumatic childhood; it was the kind of experience that could either break one's spirit or build a will of iron.

I reflected on this thought for some time. I'd never really considered I had much, if any, control over my life and destiny, but I saw that Charles Lindbergh had made a choice, and I realized I, too, had a choice. It was my choice whether I would allow the world—which included my parents, relatives, and background—to bring me down and break my spirit, or whether I would rise above a dismal heritage and circumstances with an iron will to succeed. For at least the next ten years that statement rang in my head when life got hard. It was fortunate that I chose an unbreakable iron will, because things were to get even uglier. Looking back, I should have turned to Scripture for guidance instead of going elsewhere. God's Word should have been my strength and source for how to live my life. Scripture says, *"Thy word is a lamp unto my feet and a light unto my path"* (Psalm 119:105, kjv). And God promised,

"I will never leave thee, nor forsake thee" (Hebrew 13:5, KJV). In retrospect, I realize that promise was true, and my iron will was not of my own making, but was a gift from God. Since the day of my commitment to make Jesus my Savior and Lord of my life, He was protecting me and guiding my paths. I just did not realize it at the time.

About a year later, Mom returned to the family in Bridgeport. Although she had recovered, too much had happened between her and Dad for a true reconciliation. I do not recall my parents openly fighting or arguing in front of us, but they were not getting along. When I was twelve, Dad left the family for good, and my mom had another mental episode. The State of Washington Children's Services moved in and my siblings and I were split up again. I went to an aunt's house for a short period of time before being made a ward of the State of Washington and sent to a group home in nearby Okanogan. The home was primarily comprised of delinquent children. The foster care system was not as developed then as it is today, and there were not many options for children in my situation. My sisters and I were good kids and did not get in trouble, but neither Dad nor Mom had parents or relatives who were willing to take us. I spent the rest of my childhood in the foster care system, until I was emancipated at the age of eighteen.

Only one of my foster parents attended church, so, for those six years, I seldom went to church. After my emancipation and until I was in my mid-twenties, I had very limited, sporadic contact with my sisters and parents. It was me and my iron will against the world.

Deep inside, I knew God was present, but I was not relying on Him. It seemed to me He had not done such a

great job so far. Of course, I was wrong. It's like the poem
Footprints in the Sand:

> One night a man had a dream. He dreamed he
> was walking along the beach with the Lord. Across
> the sky flashed scenes from his life. For each scene,
> he noticed two sets of footprints in the sand: One
> belonging to him, and the other to the Lord.
>
> When the last scene of his life flashed before
> him, he looked back at the footprints in the sand.
> He noticed that many times along the path of his life
> there was only one set of footprints. He also noticed
> that it happened at the very lowest and saddest times
> of his life.
>
> This really bothered him and he questioned the
> Lord about it: "Lord, You said that once I decided
> to follow You, You'd walk with me all the way. But
> I have noticed that during the most troublesome
> times in my life, there is only one set of footprints.
> I don't understand why, when I needed You most,
> You would leave me."
>
> The Lord replied: "My son, My precious child, I
> love you and I would never leave you. During your
> times of trial and suffering, when you see only one
> set of footprints, it was then that I carried you."
> — Carolyn Joyce Carty

I now know that despite my lack of acknowledgment,
God was carrying me along and watching over me through
those years. I know this is true because I was His and He
wasn't going to let me go. I had His Word on it:

For this is the will of My Father, that everyone who beholds the Son and believes in Him may have eternal life; and I Myself will raise him up on the last day. (John 6:40, NASB)

School Years

I was not a naturally good or gifted student. I was bright and tried hard, but schoolwork did not come easily. However, I was mechanically inclined. I recall when I was five years old, a couple of the light switches in our house were not working. I was aware of the power of electricity, as I had many times stuck things in the sockets and watched them burn, but my mechanical bent was more powerful than my fear, and I unscrewed the receptacles, tore them apart, and figured out how to fix them. I had them reassembled and reinstalled before my parents knew about it. I did this all without turning the power off, electrocuting myself, or paying union dues.

My dad came home from work and, out of habit, flipped the light switch. He was surprised when the light came on and asked Mom who had fixed it. I did not want to get in trouble, so at first I did not confess. Eventually I told Dad that I had done it, but he did not believe me. I had to prove it to him by reenacting the whole process and showing him how I had done it. Obviously impressed, they had me tested, and it was determined I was somewhat of a mechanical genius at age five. Of course, aptitude is one thing; using it and developing it is another. It was recommended that I be enrolled in a special school, but we were poor, so nothing ever came of it.

Because of my mechanical genius, all of my teachers in grade school loved me. I would always fix anything broken in the classroom. If there was a task that required tools, diagrams that needed to be deciphered, or something needed to be constructed, I was their star student. However, if reading or spelling was necessary, I usually found an excuse to fix something. In fact, I really did not know how to read very well until the fifth grade.

My first male teacher was my fifth grade teacher, Mr. Koch, at Terrace Elementary School in Arlington, California. My math and mechanical skills did not impress him as much as they had my female teachers; he wanted me to read and spell. I was way behind my other classmates in my reading and spelling skills, and Mr. Koch knew it would be too frustrating for both of us for him to spend class time helping me get caught up.

One day after school, he sat me down and told me I was not successful at covering up my lack of reading and spelling skills.

He asked me, "Marshall, what do you want to do when you grow up?"

I replied, "I want to be an astronaut."

"Do you think astronauts need to know how to read and spell?"

"Probably not. They just need to know how to fly, fix things, and figure out math problems." Having seen so many photographs of astronauts and rocket ships, I spoke with confidence.

"Marshall, you are much brighter than all of the other students," Mr. Koch confidently said, pointing at me as he spoke. "From now on, instead of participating in the regular class work, I want you to build the class a rocket ship."

"That's a great idea, Mr. Koch!" I nodded with enthusiasm.

"The only requirements are that you have to come up with a written plan, including drawings, periodically brief the class on your progress, and document everything you do. I will help you a little, but I want you to do as much as possible on your own." Mr. Koch was also enthusiastic—but his eyes were serious.

I eagerly agreed. My dad was a tool designer and draftsman in the aeronautical industry, and he had taught me some drawing and drafting skills, so this was going to be fun—and a cinch.

Mr. Koch knew what he was doing. He found something that would motivate me to realize I did need to know how to read and spell, even to be an astronaut. I soon discovered it was critical for me to read the books in the library about rocket ships before I could make one; just looking at the exciting pictures was not enough information. My briefing presentations to the class also required organization and proper spelling. Unfortunately, Dad's financial situation had deteriorated, our house and car were being repossessed, and we skipped out of town in the middle of the night, moving to Banning, California. I didn't complete the rocket ship project or the fifth grade. However, in the few months I was working on the rocket project, I did get my reading skills to near fifth grade level. Thanks to Mr. Koch, I enjoy reading today. I still struggle with spelling, but I'm managing, thanks to the spell checker on my computer.

I continued to feel I was in survival mode all through high school. Being a foster kid was bad enough; to emphasize that lowly status, I had no nice or new clothes, and no family to come to school events. I worked part-time jobs for spending money and to save for college, so I did not participate in most of the school's extracurricular activities. In addition, I stopped growing in the seventh grade.

All through grade school, I was of average, if not above average, height and weight. But by age twelve I stopped growing. I was just over five-foot-two and weighed 115 pounds. When I graduated from high school, I was exactly the same. Everyone in high school—including the girls— was bigger than me, which didn't help my confidence. (At nineteen, during boot camp in the Navy, I started making up for lost time, and by the time I was twenty-eight, I was five foot eleven and about fifty pounds heavier.)

In my classes, I usually got A's in subjects requiring logic such as algebra, geometry, advanced algebra, pre-calculus, physics, chemistry, and shop, but struggled with classes requiring memorization. I managed to graduate with a B average from Chelan High School in 1969, and was on my way to the University of Washington in Seattle, with the goals of getting a degree in electrical engineering and enrolling in Air Force ROTC.

I was now eighteen, emancipated from the State of Washington and on my own. Finally, my life was going the way I wanted. I would go to college, become an Air Force pilot, then an astronaut, and maybe retire as an airline pilot.

All of the other details—wife and family included—would just fall into place. What could possibly stop me now? I was about to find out.

As part of my Air Force physical, they checked my eyesight.

"Mr. Alexander, the vision in your right eye is a perfect 20/20, but unfortunately your left eye is 20/40," the doctor said.

I knew right away what that meant. No one could be a pilot in the United States Air Force without perfect vision. I was devastated.

To add to the devastation, even though my parents had not been responsible for me for the past six years, I now needed their signature for my financial aid. Of course, I did not know this until midway through my first semester in college. My mom did not qualify to sign because she was "just a housewife," and my dad refused to sign because he thought he would somehow be held financially obligated for my education. The papers clearly indicated it was for financial aid—scholarships and grants, not loans—yet he would not sign, so my financial aid was cut off. Also, the Vietnam War was in full swing, and the draft lottery system was in effect. With the way my luck was going, I figured my lottery number would soon be selected, I'd be drafted, and get killed as an army private in Vietnam. Wanting to have at least some control over where I'd die, I joined the Navy in December of 1969.

CHAPTER 5

My First Attempts at Flight

YET THOSE WHO WAIT FOR THE LORD WILL GAIN NEW
STRENGTH; THEY WILL MOUNT UP WITH WINGS LIKE EAGLES,
THEY WILL RUN AND NOT GET TIRED, THEY WILL WALK AND
NOT BECOME WEARY. (ISAIAH 40:31, NASB)

I have never had a headache or migraine in my life. However, I have been knocked unconscious eight times: five of those incidents happening before I reached the age of seven. My mom thought I was a regular kamikaze kid. Evidently, my fascination with flying began at an early age, and my first attempts at flight were self-propelled. At four and five years old, equipped with my Superman T-shirt and cape, I'd "fly" off our elevated front porch in Santa Monica, California. I couldn't say how the flights went; all I remember was waking up in a bright hospital room, seeing people staring down at me, and spotting evidence of vomit on my Superman costume and in the pan next to me.

My mom thinks that I probably damaged something in my head that is necessary to allow for headaches.

At age six, I shot my water-propelled rocket on top of the two-story apartment building next to our house. It was one of those rockets that you pumped up with water, released the plunger, and watched to see how high it would go. It just so happened that right next to the apartment building was a tall palm tree with ready-made foot and handholds all the way up to the level of the apartment building roof. The last thing I remember is walking on the roof, admiring all of the cool antennas, guy wires, and swamp coolers. I have no idea what happened next. Once again, I woke up with bright lights in my eyes and with a bedpan next to me. Apparently, they found me on the lawn, unconscious, a few feet from the sidewalk. No broken bones, a few bruises, unconscious for a while—but no headache.

Another episode when I was knocked unconscious was not my fault. My dad was working on a small John Deere garden tractor, and I was sitting in the seat, leaning to the left, looking forward, and watching him work on the snowplow blade attached to the front of the tractor. Evidently, as my dad told it, he pulled a pin holding the large spring that helped lift the snowplow blade. The lever, operated with the left hand to raise and lower the blade, released under pressure, and came back and hit me right between the eyes. My dad said I did about two flips off the back of the tractor and landed unconscious. He thought he had killed me. This time there was no hospital or medical facility in our town, so Dad had to drive thirty minutes to the doctor. I was out for several hours. I didn't wake up to bright lights this time, as my nose was broken and both eyes were swollen shut. My eyes and face were black and blue for months, it seemed. The purple bruising and the eventual yellow tone came all the way down my neck to my chest, and I hated going to school looking that way. I looked pitiful, to say the least.

It is ironic that after I survived—unscathed—fixing the lights at the age of five, one of my last attempts at self-propelled flight was as a result of electrocution. My dad used to moonlight on weekends and evenings, laying linoleum and tile. One weekend I was helping him on a new house construction that was not supposed to have live electricity. The walls were all finished and the wiring roughed in, with wires sticking out of various boxes. I was working in the kitchen, using a serrated trowel to spread sticky black mastic on the floor. Leaning forward, I worked the mastic, inching backwards toward the walls as I went. Concentrating on my work, I managed to back myself into the laundry room—and right into a live 220-volt wire for the dryer. It shocked me in the rear, knocked me unconscious, and flung me out in the middle of the floor that I had just covered in mastic.

There I was, unconscious, stuck to the middle of the floor with linoleum mastic, when my dad came around the corner to find me. He quickly dragged me out of the house and began cleaning the mastic off of me using paint thinner or something like it so that I would be clean enough to transport to the hospital. While he was cleaning me, I regained consciousness, and was totally fine. Considering my usual pattern of waking up in the hospital, it seemed like a miracle. I recall my dad did not have a very Christian attitude toward the contractor and electrician after they nearly electrocuted his only son to death.

My First Solo Flight: June 2, 1984

My first flight instruction was out of Sunnyside, Washington. My flight instructor, the co-pastor at church, was Dr. Woods. Over a period of a few weeks and several hours of flying between airports in Sunnyside and Prosser, Washington, practicing touch-and-gos, Doc Woods surprised me by saying, "I'm going to get out of the plane. Why don't you take it to Prosser, do a touch-and-go, and fly back? I'll be monitoring the radio if you need anything."

In flying circles, you always hear stories about pilots' first solos. You hear of the excitement, the fear, and the exhilaration of being in total control of the aircraft, with only the latent reminders of your flight instruction in your head. You never know when your instructor might say the words, "Take her up; she's all yours." Well, this was the day, the hour, the minute. *She's all mine,* I thought, *but now what am I going to do?* I wondered if I really was ready and if I had flown enough hours. Of course I was ready; I just needed to do what we'd been practicing. But was I really controlling the plane all by myself during these last few flights? Or was the instructor still adding input to the controls to correct for my errors? Well, I guessed I would soon find out.

It was late afternoon, and the weather was sunny and calm, a perfect day for a first solo flight.

I radioed, "Sunnyside Ground, Cessna November 2-8-7-6-Sierra at FBO ready to taxi."

The knot in my stomach loosened slightly. I had achieved the first step of my first solo flight and was now on the runway in position for takeoff.

"Sunnyside Traffic Cessna November 2-8-7-6 Sierra ready for takeoff.

I made another radio call that I was preparing to take off from Sunnyside airport, and informed air traffic that I would be flying direct to Prosser for a touch-and-go. *Should be a quick ten-nautical mile flight,* I thought. As the wheels lifted off the runway, I knew I was totally controlling the airplane. My exhilaration was tempered by trepidation. The instructor's words, "Just fly the plane" and "You fly the plane; don't let it fly you" went through my head.

The flight to Prosser airspace was uneventful. I informed Prosser traffic that I would be entering a left downwind for Runway 25. I entered at a forty-five-degree angle at pattern altitude, just like we'd practiced, checked and cross-checked the instruments, and made sure my airspeed was good. As I crossed the threshold of Runway 25, I pulled carb heat on the Cessna 150, put on ten degrees of flaps and began my slow controlled descent. I called out left base Runway 25, and shortly after turned final for Runway 25.

Once again, I made a radio call, "Prosser traffic Cessna November 2- 8-7-6 Sierra short final Runway 25 for touch-and-go."

Everything was set up perfectly for my first solo landing. I was now at 300 feet AGL (above ground level), power off, full flaps, and set up great, when out of nowhere, a powered ultralight aircraft swung right in front of me with the intention to land! I was moving much faster than the ultralight and would overtake and run over it if I didn't think fast. I gave the plane immediate full power, took off carb heat, pulled off the flaps, and pulled back on the yoke. I barely missed hitting the ultralight. As I was leveling off and gaining airspeed, I was simultaneously talking on the radio, giving the ultralight a piece of my mind, and watching where it was taxiing. I tried to gain my composure and figure out what I was supposed to do now. Obviously, the ultralight did not have a radio, and must have never seen me; he was just out for a quick joy ride.

I did a go-around and proceeded to enter left traffic and try again. All went smoothly this time, and as I was in a high-speed taxi for takeoff again, I glanced over to the hangars to see where that ultralight had gone. It was not in sight. I've always wondered if the ultralight pilot even knew how close he had come to his final flight that day.

Now it was much later than my instructor intended, due to the near mid-air collision and go-around, and it was time to make the trip back to Sunnyside. The typical late afternoon winds had picked up and I had a substantial gusty crosswind to contend with. I hadn't practiced crosswind landings, but was forced to do one. As I entered the pattern, I could feel the wind try to move the airplane out of my normal pattern. My turn to final approach overshot the end of the runway, so I fishtailed to try to keep it lined up. I was thinking, *This is going to be great; my first full-stop landing may not be pretty.* The FBO owner and my instructor were outside watching me struggle to keep the plane lined up. My airspeed was slightly up and down as I wobbled the plane in during the final descent. I did manage to touch down in the middle of the runway, but as soon as the wheels were solidly on the ground, the plane took off toward the sidelines. I used the rudder pedals to correct, but overcorrected and went heading for the other side of the runway. After a few wild "S" turns down the runway, the airplane slowed enough for me to keep it well in control, and I taxied over to the tie-down area, where I exhaled loudly.

As soon as I got out of the airplane, the instructor wanted to know what happened over at Prosser and what took me so long. He congratulated me on my first crosswind landing, though he thought I might need to practice a few more soon. The owner of the FBO and the airplane walked around the plane to make sure it was still in one piece. He agreed that maybe I should get some crosswind training before I soloed again. Well, there's always no time like the present, so the instructor and I went up for some crosswind training and four more touch-and-go landings.

That was an exciting day—and of course made for a great first solo story. Amazingly, after some twenty-five years of flying and hundreds of landings, I have not had another near mid-air collision or an out-of-control landing as bad as that first solo crosswind landing. As a new pilot, I did not realize how close I had come to eternity that day.

CHAPTER 6

The Crash

AND THE LORD WILL CONTINUALLY GUIDE YOU,
AND SATISFY YOUR DESIRE IN SCORCHED PLACES,
AND GIVE STRENGTH TO YOUR BONES;
AND YOU WILL BE LIKE A WATERED GARDEN,
AND LIKE A SPRING OF WATER WHOSE WATERS DO NOT FAIL.
(ISAIAH 58:11, NASB)

March 16, 2007

I sensed I was near the ground, so I turned on my landing light and leaned forward to watch the trees, rocks, and cliffs pass only a few hundred feet beneath me. I remembered the two pillows in the back seat, so I reached back and placed one lengthwise in my lap. The pillow was between me and the yoke that I held tightly with my left hand, while I also held the flight yoke. I took my glasses off and set them in the passenger seat. I held the other pillow in my right hand, ready to put it in front of my face on impact. I wasn't watching the altimeter or panel anymore; I was just trying to see what was ahead and where I was going to crash.

I didn't know at what elevation I was flying now or where I was. The terrain directly under me, at least the treetops, appeared to be just a few feet below me now. It was very dark—a mountain ridge or some other terrain was coming up fast directly in front of me. I slowly gave back pressure on the yoke until the stall warning alarm went off. I tried to hold it. I kept the airplane moving as it flew slower and slower, closer and closer to the treetops.

I had taken the McCall Mountain Flying course a few summers ago when I bought a Husky tail dragger airplane, and had practiced slow-flight with both planes with the stall warning blaring. Of course, during practice, the engine was running and the prop was still adding some forward thrust and wash over the wings, adding lift.

I had previously determined I had seven to nine knots of slower indicated flight speed even after the stall warning began, giving me some leeway before the actual stall. I tried to get as slow as possible without stalling the plane, with no running engine and no additional lift. So far, so good.

It seemed I was gliding for some time, with no elevation loss, as I slowly held backpressure. All I saw were treetops just inches below me. One extra tall tree would do me in. The plane began to stall and rock around, out of control. I knew this was it. No more gliding, it was time to crash. Out of time and without really thinking it through, I pulled full back on the yoke, which wasn't much at that point, attempting to put the plane in a full stall. I put the pillow to my face and closed my eyes. I felt the plane turn sharp left and down. The plane was out of control. I had no authority over the airplane, the landing, the crash location, or the remaining seconds of my life.

Whether the last few moments of flight lasted a fraction of a second or a few seconds, I don't know. Neither did I see what was happening. My life was in God's hands. I was clutching my pillows, eyes closed, waiting and bracing for impact and a certain, quick death. I didn't hear or feel crashing, just one big, straightforward, hard impact, and then debris and cold snow brushed past my arms, which were still holding the pillows.

In an instant, all was quiet, except for the blaring squeal of my stall warning horn. I put the pillow down and turned off the master switch to silence the noise. Everything was dark, silent, and cold. I sat there in amazement.

I had never crashed an airplane—or died—before, so I didn't know what to expect. Was I dead? Alive? I was stunned that I had just crashed, and possibly survived, and that I felt no pain.

Peggy Lee's voice echoed through my confusion: *Is this all there is to an airplane crash?*

What a miracle, I thought, *if I'm actually really alive!* It was astonishing to think that I'd just crashed my airplane from 12,500 feet in the rugged Cascade wilderness, in complete darkness, and that I'd survived, apparently unhurt. *God truly does know how to fly an airplane and keep His own safe, unless this is a dream or something.* I sat and thought how I hadn't asked God to save me, but He did anyway. I didn't cry out to God for a miracle, He just provided one. I was certain I had made a pilot error that was going to cost me my life, and assumed God was ready to take me home. Evidently, He had other plans. Praise the Lord!

Survival

After a few moments, I began to realize that I was still alive, and, yes, I really had crashed. My heart sank knowing I had just destroyed my beautiful 1956 Cessna 182. It was such a pretty airplane and had always turned heads when I landed it at airports around the United States. But I was alive! I thanked God audibly with a "Thank You, Jesus," and began to assess the situation. I found the flashlight where I had left it in the side pocket of my bag and turned it on.

A snowbank was a foot from my face, not a windshield. My airplane was buried nose down in the snow with snow blocking both of the doors and windows, except the small back left-hand passenger window. My BAS shoulder harness had done its job well but was now in my lap, having pulled completely out and through the airplane roof, the bolts sheared off. I thought, *Now that was a good investment I made a few years ago.* Without the pillows and shoulder harness, I doubt that my frail body would have made it through the impact. When I tried to pull myself out of the seat, I became aware that all wasn't well. My right leg was pinned at the upper thigh between the seat and the dash. I couldn't move the seat back, and I couldn't push off on my right foot because something was wrong with it. I tried to pull and pry with my arms, but I had limited strength in my arms due to increasing severe chest pain. I thought I might have broken my right leg, right foot, and some ribs. My teeth hurt and my right jaw was stiff and creaked when I moved my mouth. I saw no blood, no lacerations, and no missing body parts, so I still thought things were not too bad.

I am not sure how long it took me to pry and wiggle out of the pilot seat, maybe ten to fifteen minutes, but eventually I made it to the small back left window. The doors and other windows were all buried in the snow making an exit impossible. The small back window on the left was badly cracked by the impact of the crash, so it was fairly easy to break out the plastic window with my left hand. My right hand and arm were now swollen from hitting the dash while holding the pillow. After breaking and pulling out all of the sharp edges of the plastic window so I would not impale myself, I thought I could climb through. I looked around with the flashlight and found everything I thought would be useful and pushed them out of the window first. It was only slightly painful to crawl out of the small window and when I landed, the cold snow actually felt good. Once I was out I turned the flashlight on and was startled when I saw blood all over the snow. I checked myself for cuts or lacerations, but found none until I realized I had cut my left hand while breaking the window out.

I stood upright for the first time next to the left wing and immediately felt a stabbing pain and tremendous heat down my right side. I fell to the snow, doubled up with the severe pain, unable to do anything but lie there for a few minutes thinking I must have internal injuries. I prayed under my breath that Jesus would get me through this. Since He had protected me this far, why would He allow me to die now?

A few seconds after my prayer, the pain went away. I stood up and pressed around on my stomach and back but didn't feel anything out of place or experience the extreme pain—at least not the pain I had felt just a few moments ago. My chest and right leg were sore, but whatever severe pain I had just felt was now gone. I chalked it up to another miracle of God within the past thirty minutes.

Now that my body was relatively intact, what about getting out of here? I quickly looked at my cell phone and saw no signal, so I pulled out my ICOM handheld transceiver and began transmitting on 121.5, which is the universal airplane emergency frequency. I heard the shrilling sound of an emergency-locating transmitter (ELT) while on 121.5 and assumed my airplane's ELT was transmitting. However, there was no response to my emergency calls.

Not knowing if anyone heard my calls, I started assessing the damage to my plane. The rear baggage door was broken open and all of my belongings were lying there, ready to be pulled out: sleeping bag, pad, overnight bag, and the emergency bag with food. Several years ago I had an extended baggage compartment installed which had a nice-sized storage compartment with a long-hinged lid. I stored additional emergency equipment there: heavy-duty space blankets, flares, cooking utensils, candles, small stove for cooking and heating water, and a Ram-Line .22-caliber pistol with a couple hundred rounds. A small backpack held dehydrated meals, another flashlight and spare batteries, emergency whistle, signal mirror, aluminum foil, and a bunch of other things that I thought might be useful if I ever got stranded. I knew if I could get to the things I had stored, and my injuries were not any worse than they appeared to be, I could last for days out here.

Unfortunately, the adrenaline in my body had begun to wear off and my pain started to increase. I was now barely able to breathe. With each breath I felt sharp pains knifing me in the middle of my chest. My right leg was useless and swelling. Due to the chest pain, I could not crawl in far enough through the baggage door to unfasten the normal turn fasteners to get to the additional storage. To survive, I had to have my emergency gear. My mechanical brain found a solution that my injured body could carry out: I pulled out the long pin that secured the hinges and took the whole door off. Crawling back into the compartment as far as I could, I pulled everything down to my feet, although the pain prevented me from reaching some of the items I wanted, like the stove, fuel, and my .22-caliber rifle.

I could tell I was on a very steep mountainside in a small snowfield with a sheer rock cliff behind me, and trees all around. I crawled out and made a little nest in the snow using the left wing, which was at a sharp angle and knifed into the steep snowfield. It became a strong support so I would not roll down the mountain. I laid out my sleeping pad, sleeping bag and pillows, flannel blankets, space blankets, and emergency gear in an organized fashion, anticipating being unable to move from the spot and wanting to have everything I needed within easy reach. I began nibbling on a power bar to keep my carbohydrate and heat levels up, and climbed into my warm nest. I didn't crawl in the sleeping bag, but unzipped it and lay on top of it with part of it over me, then piled on the flannel blankets and space blankets. I was afraid if I crawled in a zipped-up sleeping bag and the soreness and stiffness increased, I would not be able to get out.

Now in relative comfort, I laid my head down on the pillows and changed the ICOM frequency to 122.75, the common plane-to-plane frequency, and began transmitting in the blind, hoping some nearby airplane would hear my

The pictures of the airplane crash scene on these two pages were taken by the Civil Air Patrol airplane a few minutes after Marshall's rescue.

CRASH SITE

Above: *Panel of crashed plane.* Below: *The recovered plane.*

Above: *Marshall, one month after the crash.*
Below: *At the computer, working on the story.*

distress call. After several minutes without a response, I went to the satellite phone. Once again, no signal. I continued to alternate frequencies on the ICOM between 121.5 and 122.75, still without a response. I heard the satellite phone make a noise, so I looked at it and saw it had found a signal. I dialed my home number and got our answering machine. It was probably around 10:45 P.M. and everyone was asleep at home, thinking I was safely in Eugene visiting my sister. I left a message, telling my wife and family I was alive, I had crashed my airplane, and did not know exactly where I was. I then dialed 911. Just as the connection began, the signal went dead. Lost signal! Over the next several hours that would be the scenario repeated again and again— limited satellite phone coverage, brief conversations barely long enough to identify myself and indicate I'd crashed an airplane, then a lost signal.

Using my flashlight, I could tell I was in a deep ravine that caused my signal to the satellites to be very weak. It was definitely one of the more frustrating parts of the evening. I would stare at the satellite phone screen sometimes for thirty minutes or more, watching for a connection, then immediately begin dialing, often losing the signal before I even completed the call. I had many phone numbers pre-programmed in the phone but did not try calling friends or relatives, only my wife, 911, and Center.

As it turned out, Center was Houston Center in Texas—probably because that is where the satellite phone signal originates. I'm sure it was a shock for Center in Texas to get a call from a downed airplane in Oregon. My basic message was: "I've crashed, I'm alive, please start looking for me." I wanted to know what frequency I should be transmitting on to reach any rescue efforts. After a few calls to Center where I was cut off before I could explain my situation, I gave up on them.

After an hour or so of this, I decided to climb back in the plane through the window and get my brown flight guide, which would have local tower and flight service frequencies. I was hoping as well to thumb through the tabs to see if I could remember any other emergency information. The crawl was very painful, but I did find the book—and my camera. After I had crawled out again, I tried to take a few pictures of the situation. I found that the flash on the camera was broken. I could have used it for signaling, but the normal short lens was broken off. The telephoto worked fine but I could not focus in on short-range objects, which at night was all I saw. I tried to work on it in the dark while holding the flashlight but I could not figure it out. Cold, pain, fatigue, and frustration didn't help.

After a few more calls to Globalstar 911, the receptionist and I began recognizing each other's voices and I no longer had to explain everything over and over again. Instead, I spoke directly, quickly, and to the point. I also managed to get a call through to my wife's cell phone. Once again, there was no answer, so I left another message before losing the signal. Throughout the night I was never very cold unless I purposefully crawled out of my nest. My right foot and ankle were swollen to the size of a grapefruit and hurt badly, so I put it in the snow bank and iced it down. This helped the pain and swelling, but also thoroughly chilled me. I did not take my tennis shoe off, knowing if I did I would never get it on again. If help didn't arrive within a few days, I knew I might need to walk out of there, or at least get to the top of the ravine to get better satellite reception. I was conscious of potential shock and hypothermia, and now and then I would stop and assess what I was doing, thinking to see if all was well. I felt confident I was not losing it, except, periodically, I wanted to kill the satellite phone. A few more bites of the power bar helped.

Twice during the early hours of the incident, I heard and spotted an airplane overhead, off in the direction of what I thought was north-northwest. I could see their strobes and running lights. Both times I set off a flare to signal them, and keyed 122.75 and transmitted in the blind, but without response. I assumed they were transit airplanes flying to Portland. With only one flare left, I knew I had to be certain and use it when the airplane was closer and able to see it.

I continued to see airplanes overhead throughout the night and began using two of my flashlights for signaling. I thought I had another packet of three flares in the plane, but I was too sore to try to retrieve them at this time. I figured if I were really desperate, I would take the pain and look for them. I also had a small black case of emergency supplies I had stored behind my pilot seat that had, among other things, a small battery-powered strobe light, but I could not find it during my earlier probes in the cockpit. Once again, I thought if I had to, I would crawl through the window again or try taking the back seat out to retrieve more gear.

Often I just stared up into the heavens and admired the bright stars while looking for airplanes overhead. I prayed and sang praise songs to Jesus, my Lord and Savior, at the top of my lungs, which was not much at that point. I could not take big breaths, but I wanted God to hear my praises—off-key, garbled, and broken as they were. I knew God loved me and for some reason spared my life that night. In the dark, silent night, I asked Him why. My wife and I had eight children and nine grandchildren (twelve at this writing, with one more on the way) to influence and continue to train up in the way of the Lord. Was that it? Or was the crash a wake-up call to be more zealous than ever in sharing my faith and in witnessing with more boldness? With just God and me alone on the mountain during the night hours, I was hoping for a revelation. I did not get any overwhelming impression from God. But I was hopeful we would continue to communicate and figure it out. But maybe I needed to get off this mountain first.

After awhile I made contact with my wife on the satellite phone. Our conversations were reassuring and brief. Once again, I wanted to know what frequency I should use to transmit with the ICOM transceiver if rescue efforts were near. When she told me I should use 123.1, I verified that with her because I had never heard of that frequency used for any purpose. She was in contact with the FAA in Saratoga, Florida, and that was what they told her. Why Saratoga, Florida, and why that frequency? I didn't have time to argue. From then on, that was the only frequency I transmitted on. After four hours of periodic transmissions, the battery on the ICOM was low, so I turned it off now and again to conserve the power. The satellite phone was also indicating a low battery, so I was hesitant about using it, too.

I began to believe that my airplane's ELT was not transmitting—or at least not strongly enough to make contact with the outside world. The shrill sound on the ICOM when dialed to 121.5 might not have been my airplane, but an internal signal—I couldn't remember. I tried to open the compartment where the ELT was stored to manually activate it, but my chest injury prevented me from having the strength to pull the hinge wire out or break into the compartment. I pulled and screamed at the top of my lungs while pulling and pushing, hoping the old Kung Fu yell would do the trick, but to no avail. I also thought if I could climb back into the cabin, I could manually hit the switch if it were still there, or try the master switch again to see if the GPS was still working. That was the one thing I thought and rethought while lying in the snow, *Why didn't I just look down at the GPS and see if it was still working and see what my coordinates were?* It sure would have saved everyone a lot of frantic rescue work if I could just have given them my exact location. To ease my frustration with myself, I told myself that maybe it didn't work anyway.

I figured God didn't save me from the crash just to die on the mountain. I was as excited as a kid to get to use all of my cool emergency equipment I had carried around for years—and had to convince my wife to let me buy. Actually, she let me buy almost everything for the plane if it meant safety, but she had been questioning the $65.00 a month satellite phone bill, since I'd never used the phone. As it turned out, the satellite phone is probably what got the rescue efforts moving so quickly. I later learned its signal was triangulated to locate me on the mountainside. The authorities knew that my plane had gone down in the middle of the night, in the heart of the Cascade Mountains, but after we lost radio contact, they assumed I had crashed and was dead. They were in no hurry to initiate a recovery search that night. After I had made the satellite phone calls to Houston Center, Globalstar 911, and Judy, word was out that I was alive, injured, and needed immediate rescue. Without the satellite phone, I might have been waiting for days before anyone came looking for the airplane—and my corpse.

CHAPTER 7

Judy's Story

EVEN THOUGH I WALK THROUGH THE VALLEY OF THE
SHADOW OF DEATH, I WILL FEAR NO EVIL,
FOR YOU ARE WITH ME; YOUR ROD AND YOUR STAFF,
THEY COMFORT ME. (PSALM 23:4, NIV)

Crash Day

On the day of the crash, Marshall and I had been dealing with problems with two of our children. As parents, it seems your job of training your children is never done. We decided to go outside and do some yard work as a respite from our kids' issues.

Our home is situated on twelve acres in Klamath Falls, Oregon. With about thirty to forty big trees and a lake behind us, I sometimes feel as though I live in a large park. Early in the morning, the sun rises and the wind blows softly in my face and I just sit and enjoy the view of the lake. *Heaven on Earth* is a fitting description. Our property is not low maintenance by any stretch of the imagination, but it is definitely something Marshall and I enjoy working on together.

When we bought the property, the house was already there. It had been foreclosed on and been empty for over a year. It was formerly a bed-and-breakfast and was one of the fancier houses in Klamath Falls when it was built in 1992. It has five bedrooms and four-and-a-half bathrooms, and is easily 5,000 square feet. By the time we purchased it, though, the two winters it sat empty had taken a toll. Ever since we moved into the house seven years ago, Marshall and I have spent countless hours fixing it up. Working outside on the twelve acres and inside on house repairs has kept us both in good shape.

I was blessed to be able to stay home and care for our eight children, as well as about twenty-two foster children through the years. We always had a lot of projects going on at once—and still do. We enjoyed everything from working together in our mini-orchard of fruit trees, to raising cattle, to building a fancy new horse barn.

We were outside on our respite when we got the call about Marshall's sister Debby. Her husband said she had just been taken to the hospital with a possible heart attack. Naturally, Marshall wanted to go be with her and immediately started making flight plans. I guess with everything that was going on around the house and the yard work that needed to be done, I was a little miffed at Marshall, and not very supportive of his leaving. I did not have a very Christ-like attitude, but finally I told him, "How about you just fly up and see your sister, and I will drive up with the kids in the car later?" Marshall agreed.

As he began to get ready for the trip, in my heart I did not want him to go, but I knew that he needed to and that he would be a blessing to his sister. He started all of his usual flight preparations, mainly checking the weather, and it looked like it would be a nice flight. Then he left for the airport.

I usually ask Marshall to call as soon as he lands, but I, in my miffed state, forgot to ask. When he did not call, it was easy for me to surmise that he must have hurried straight to the hospital and had not had time to call me. I tried not to let it bother me, and I decided that it was best to get some rest and call him in the morning. I said a prayer for him and went to bed.

The next thing I knew, I heard a man's voice downstairs. It was someone leaving a message on our answering machine. Who could it be at this hour? Was something wrong with Marshall's sister? When I went down, I could see the answering machine light blinking. As I was about to listen to the message the phone started ringing.

"Hello?" I answered.

It was the FAA calling:

"Are you Judy Alexander?"

"Yes," I said.

"Is your husband Marshall Alexander?"

"Yes," I said.

"Was he flying his plane N6462 Alpha tonight?"

"Yes, what is going on?" I asked.

"We got a report that a plane went down. Do you know where he was going?"

I said, "Yes, to Eugene, Oregon."

They said they would get right back to me.

My heart fell. This wasn't good. The FAA does not call in the middle of the night for no real reason.

I prayed to God to please help him, and help me know what to do. My mind was going a hundred miles an hour. *Stay calm, Judy. You need to get help for Marshall.*

As soon as I hung up the phone, it rang again. This time it was Bill Hancock, the airport operations manager from Klamath Falls. He asked me the same questions the FAA asked, but he also asked if Marshall had any emergency equipment on the plane. I was thankful that Marshall always had a big bag of equipment on his plane. He had spent a small fortune through the years and had bought every piece of emergency equipment available. Mr. Hancock then told me they would do everything they could to find him and said to call him if I heard any more news.

I hung the phone up and saw the answering machine light still blinking. I pressed the button. It was Marshall's voice. He said:

"I've crashed. I'm alive, but I don't know where I am and you don't get the life insurance." Ah, same old Marshall!

Then the phone went dead.

This is how our phone messages went for the next eight hours or so: a few seconds of phone connection every thirty or forty minutes.

During one brief conversation, I told him everyone was here. In typical Marshall fashion, he said, "Why don't you make everybody hot chocolate and marshmallows?" Actually, he probably just wanted some hot chocolate for himself.

In another conversation, I asked him, "Where are you, Marshall?" He said, "Hanging on the side of a mountain." I could hardly believe that he was still so witty and in bright spirits considering what had just happened to him. I thought, "At least he still has his sense of humor ... that must be a good sign."

I called Bill Hancock back and told him I got a short message from Marshall on his satellite phone saying he was alive, but he did not know where he was. Knowing that Marshall had crashed and was alive and out in the cold changed the rescue plan totally.

Mr. Hancock wanted to know Marshall's satellite phone number. I did not know it. Marshall had always called me from it; I had never called him. I was running through the house going through all the Globalstar papers to find the phone number. I could not find it. I even tried calling Globalstar, but it was too early in the morning for them to be answering their phones.

Then I thought of Russell. He was Marshall's friend and had previously borrowed the phone. He had an unlisted number, so I sped over to his house and pounded on his front door to wake him up.

"Russell, Marshall has crashed his plane!" I exclaimed.

"What? Where is he?" Russell inquired.

"We don't know. That's why I'm here. Do you know the phone number to Marshall's satellite phone?" I answered quickly.

"No, no I don't. I only called out on it. I'm so sorry," Russell explained in disappointment.

Feeling defeated, I drove back home.

Thankfully, Mr. Hancock called often to update us on the rescue efforts. I, in turn, would tell him about my brief conversations with Marshall. At this point, they still didn't know where Marshall was. Without the coordinates, it was like looking for a needle in a haystack.

By now enough time had passed, and back east Globalstar answered their phone. I finally found out the number to Marshall's satellite phone. Now if we could only get a connection, we might have an easier time locating him.

Before long, the Sheriff's Department was calling to say that Sheriff Tim Evinger was starting to put together a search and rescue crew. We believed that Marshall was in a wilderness area, which meant they would have to attempt a rescue on foot. When I relayed this information to Marshall, he said that based on what he could see, he didn't think they would be able to get to him on foot.

Somewhere in all of this, I managed to call my two adult daughters, our pastor, family members, including my sister Linda, and my mom to get prayers going.

Judy's Sister, Linda

Hear my prayer, O LORD! And let my cry for help come to Thee. (Psalm 102:1, NASB)

Judy called me sometime after midnight to tell me that Marshall had crashed his plane on a snowy mountain and "… to please pray that he would be found and not freeze to death." I immediately started praying. Afterward, I thought of my sister and what she must be going through. She and her daughters must be so worried. I quickly got dressed, jumped in the car, and drove over to their house.

When I arrived at the house, I found my sister on the phone trying to assist those who were desperately trying to figure out Marshall's location. They were using all the tools they had available to them: satellite, GPS, and the calls from Marshall. Judy was on autopilot; she was methodically doing what needed to be done.

Finally, they were able to pick up the signal from Marshall's satellite phone. Rescue planes went up and began flying in the area where they believed Marshall had crashed. The whole house was ecstatic when we learned one of the airplanes had spotted a flare. Praise the Lord! It was the news we had been waiting for. The next challenge would be to figure out how to get to him. He was in an area that was too steep and dense for nighttime rescue. We would have to wait until daylight.

On the final phone call we received from Marshall, he was shivering and told us he knew that he needed to fix himself something to eat, but that meant making his way back to the plane, which he didn't want to do because it "hurt to move." We were encouraging him to try to make his way back to the plane when the phone suddenly went dead.

Something happens to a person when they come face-to-face with the possibility of losing a family member. The things that are important become clearer. Instantly, I was comforted by the fact that Marshall knew God, and better yet, God knew Marshall. I knew if he died, he would be in the presence of God. That night the best thing we could do was pray and trust God to answer our prayers. Even if His answer was not what we had hoped for, He was still worthy of our affection. *"Though He slay me, yet will I trust Him"* (Job 13:15, NKJV).

Judy's Son, Cody

> *In my distress I called upon the LORD, and cried to my God for help; He heard my voice out of His temple, And my cry for help before Him came into His ears.* (Psalm 18:6, NASB)

I was asleep when the phone started ringing. My sister, Michelle, was calling to tell me that Dad had crashed his plane. I thought, *Oh, God, please don't take my dad.* There were a thousand things running through my head: *Does he know how much I love him, and how much he means to me and my family? Does he know I'm sorry for the things I did when I was younger? How is Mom?*

I did not want to wait for the rescue crews; I wanted to go find him myself, right then. I immediately went to be with my mom. It seemed like everyone they knew was there. When I finally heard my dad's voice, it was the best sound I had heard all night. I was so glad that his spirits were high. He told my mom that he was lying in the snow singing to God every praise song he could remember.

CHAPTER 8

Rescued

PEACE I LEAVE WITH YOU; MY PEACE I GIVE TO YOU; NOT AS
THE WORLD GIVES, DO I GIVE TO YOU. LET NOT YOUR HEART
BE TROUBLED, NOR LET IT BE FEARFUL.
(JOHN 14:27, NASB)

Other than the aches and pains from the crash, I was feeling comfortable with my situation. God had prepared me for circumstances similar to this through many past experiences. Over the course of my life, I had spent many hours in the outdoors and the woods. During my Navy years and in college, I started backpacking and enjoying the serenity of God's creation. I also took up downhill skiing with a Navy buddy. Most of the time it was just God, the mountains, and me. After college I met a good Christian friend—the same Christian friend I mentioned earlier who owned the Bible bookstore—who introduced me to mountain climbing and to other Christians who enjoyed backpacking and mountain climbing. As a result, over the years, either with them or solo, I have climbed most all of the major, and some minor, mountains in the

Northwest. Some of the bigger mountains were Mount Rainier, Mount Hood, Mount Shasta, Glacier Peak, Mount Olympus, Mount Adams, and Mount Baker.

In the early eighties, I worked in northeastern Oregon in the little town of Joseph. For several years the area developed a small ski area called Ferguson Ridge. It was getting to the size and popularity that made many think it was time to have a ski patrol. About this same time, there was an avalanche in an area where many people cross-country skied. Unfortunately, the avalanche killed several people, in part, because there was no avalanche rescue system in place. Soon after this tragedy, several people in the community who loved the outdoors, skiing, and helping people—myself included—formed a combined Nordic and Alpine (cross-country and downhill) ski patrol and joined the National Ski Patrol system. We trained and skied with the Anthony Lakes and Spout Springs ski areas, as well as Ferguson Ridge.

On a few Nordic training exercises, we cross-country skied miles out into the mountains and spent two to three days building snow caves in which to sleep, and in rescuing each other from simulated skiing and avalanche accidents. The idea was to go out into the snow in the middle of the winter, sometimes with a full pack of gear, sometimes with just a fanny pack and a few essentials, and be able to make a temporary shelter for oneself and a potential victim— and actually spend a few nights in the snowy shelter, just for fun.

In more recent years, I've taught two of my boys about snow camping. Crater Lake is not far from Klamath Falls and it is a beautiful scenic area, both in the summer and winter. In the winter it gets 500 inches of snow, which is great for cross-country skiing and building snow caves. The boys and I have cross-country skied in the woods near the rim of the lake, pitched a tent, and then built a snow cave for our kitchen and also just for the experience. It takes effort and a survival mind-set for these activities, but in the end, we call it fun.

With this background, camping in the snow on the side of a mountain was something I was comfortable with. When and how I was to get rescued, however, was something else. First, somebody would have to locate me, and then they would have to get me out of here. The odds were against me on both.

My best bet was to try to attract attention at night, using the lights I had available, since attracting help in the daylight hours in the snow is difficult. I was hopeful someone would be looking for me from the air at night or, if they were not specifically looking for me, at least in the pitch-black night my flares and flashlights might attract their attention.

With that thought in mind, every now and again I would see an airplane overhead and would turn the flashlights on and shine them in the direction of the airplanes flying overhead. Again, I saw a plane flying far north of me. I began signaling with the flashlight and the plane seemed to turn toward me. Flash! Flash! Flash! Did they see my signal? The plane continued toward me. My mind raced. This could be it! Should I use my last flare? Where exactly was my last flare?

My injured chest was right up against the left wing that had knifed into the snow three or four feet. There was a one-inch gap between the snow and the underside of the wing surface. Unfortunately, during the dark night hours, my last flare fell down that gap between the wing and the snow. I tried to retrieve it a few times, but the pain was too great. My chest hurt badly and my breathing was quick and shallow because of the sharp, stabbing pain. Isaiah 41:10 popped into my head: *"Fear not, for I am with you; be not dismayed; for I am your God: I will strengthen you; yea, I will help you; yea, I will uphold you with the right hand of my righteousness."*

Now, knowing that the airplane appeared to be flying toward me, I had the extra incentive to make one final push to reach the flare. I stretched and twisted awkwardly, but it was still two or three inches out of my reach. The plane was much closer now; this could be my last chance! I took the biggest, deepest breath I could, yelled, and shoved my hand as far in as I could. I heard a loud thump in my chest and felt a tremendous sharp pain, but I grabbed the flare. Although out of breath and panting, I rested my arms over the wing and set off the flare. Within seconds, the airplane flew directly over me and began circling. I was found! A tremendous feeling of warm relief washed over my entire body. Even though I was ready to meet my Maker, I was thrilled to know that I would once again get the chance to work in the yard with my wife and see my kids.

At least half of the challenge was now met. I was located, and they knew I was alive and at least well enough to frantically wave a flashlight in the middle of the night. But how were they going to rescue me? Even though I did not know exactly where I had crashed, I knew from my past flying experiences over this area that it was very rough terrain with roads that were not maintained in the winter. I wasn't sure how far away a road might be from my location, but I was pretty sure it would not be plowed and was probably impassable in the winter. Snowmobiles could be used in some areas, but even their use was questionable in this steep, rough terrain. Were I in a wilderness area, no motorized vehicles or machines would be allowed in—not even for a life-or-death rescue.

In one of my brief satellite phone calls to Judy, after she had been told that I had been spotted, she mentioned that a ground rescue was on the way and that they would reach me in a couple of hours. Once again, I reflected back on my own experiences with the ski patrol on mountain rescues and was very skeptical that anyone could reach me in a few hours of cross-country skiing or using snowshoes, as I was in extremely rugged and treacherous terrain. I told Judy that I was fine up there until morning, so people should not be risking their lives in the middle of the night to try to get to me. Of course, I did not have a voice in the rescue operation, and Judy assured me that rescue was on the way.

The rescue team did not arrive "in a couple of hours," as promised. Hour after hour, alone, injured, and in pain, I waited. The rescuers took another five hours to reach me— but what a very blessed five hours it was. They spotted me at 3:30 A.M. and rescued me at 8:00 A.M., and all during those hours I praised God. I knew He was going to finish the work He had started in me. He continually comforted me with the Scriptures that came to the forefront of my heart and mind: *You intended to harm me, **but God intended it for good** to accomplish what is now being done, the saving of many lives* (Genesis 50:20, NIV, emphasis mine).

And, *"For I, the* LORD *your God, will hold your right hand, saying to you, 'Fear not: I will help you'"* (Isaiah 41:13, NKJV).

For the remaining hours of the night and morning, I heard and saw a single-engine search plane circling overhead. The first pilot circled above me for over three hours, and then flew off when another plane appeared and began circling. The newcomer then began the slow circling, staying with me until he was relieved by still another plane. I have now learned those planes were from the Civil Air Patrol and were manned by Scott Bakker, Jim Metcalff, and Tom Moore. Scott Bakker is out of Brookings, Oregon, and was the one who first spotted me. He was the angel that stayed in the sky for over three hours, just circling, giving me comfort with the drone of his airplane engine. In the meantime, I continued singing to God every praise song I could remember:

Lord, I lift your name on high,
Lord, I love to sing your praises;
I'm so glad you're in my life,
I'm so glad you came to save us.
You came from Heaven to Earth, to show the way,
From the Earth to the Cross, my debt to pay,
From the Cross to the grave, from the grave to the sky,
Lord, I lift your name on high.

The Marshall J. Alexander of March 16, 2007, died aboard N6462A and was reborn March 17, 2007.

"God, I do not know what you have in store for me, but what I do know is you must have spared my life for something new and different. Use me, Lord. My life is in your hands."

His grace saved me many years ago, early in life, when I received Him as my Lord and Savior, and His grace saved me once again in the plane crash.

Eventually, the sun came up and I could see the terrain that surrounded me. Just as I had thought, it was very steep and rugged. From where I sat with the airplane, I realized the miracle of where I had landed—and it was more of a landing than a crash. Rocks, granite cliffs, and trees surrounded me in the small snowfield where I found myself. The snowfield opened up below me and to the east, but my location was a miracle. How did I not hit something harder than soft snow? God truly is the best copilot you can ever have when you have closed your eyes and you're clutching your pillows, waiting for the crash that will launch you into the final moments of your life.

I was also very curious to find out how a ground rescue team was going to get to me, and then how they would get me out. In a downhill ski area, when skiers were injured, we would put them on toboggans and ski them down the mountain to the warm, waiting lodge and first aid station. The toboggans were either brought up to the top of the mountains with a ski lift or pulled up with snowmobiles. Dragging a rescue toboggan though this terrain would be virtually impossible. So how was I going to be rescued?

Judy

Back at the house, we were antsy. All we wanted was to have Marshall rescued, but it seemed like it was taking forever. We prayed and prayed—and then prayed some more. Time passed so slowly, and we were desperate to hear any good news. Finally, Sheriff Evinger said he was going to make a call to get Marshall off of the mountain immediately. I don't know if his call was what worked, but in the next ten minutes, about 3:30 A.M., I got another call that Marshall had been spotted. The Civil Air Patrol had been out looking for him. They were going over the route they thought he would have flown when they spotted a downed plane and saw movement. This was no easy feat in the winter at night when everything looks white.

As soon as I got off the phone and told everyone that they had spotted Marshall, exhilaration broke out in the house. We all started talking. Where was he? Could they see if he was all right? How were they going to get him off the mountain? We were all overjoyed and thankful to God for His mercy.

Soon after, Marshall was able to call me and say there was a single-engine search plane overhead—an angel in the sky. He knew he was going to be okay. Now that they had located him, they could get the coordinates to the rescue team so they could figure out how to get to him. At that time, the rescue team still thought they could get to Marshall by foot, and were trying to get enough crew members and the right equipment together.

As time went on, they could see they would not be able to get to him on foot. The terrain was too steep and rugged, with granite cliffs and trees surrounding him. They made a decision to go in with a helicopter, but they needed to wait until the sun was up so they could see well enough.

I kept telling Marshall they were trying to work everything out so they could get to him—it would just be a little longer.

Marshall

The sweet sound of the drone of a helicopter came at 7:50 A.M. My heart began to beat faster as I realized this was the rescue. The answer to my curious rescue question was not a ground rescue, but a helicopter. I flew into the mountain ravine, and I was going to fly out. The downdraft of the helicopter's prop wash made me shiver with cold, but I did not care one bit, at least for the first few minutes.

As I waited for something to happen above me, I began to pull some smaller, but most precious belongings out of the plane and put them in a pile at my feet. I had my laptop computer, camera, briefcase with the *Evidence Bible* and hundreds of *The Way of the Master* Bible tracts, and the satellite phone. After waiting through the night for some sort of a rescue, it seemed to take forever for the helicopter to actually do something other than hover above me. I was now the coldest I had been all night, and I was thinking of crawling back in the sleeping bag when the side door of the helicopter opened. My heart began to beat faster once again as I realized it was time to be rescued.

An Army National Guardsman was lowered on what looked like a three-pronged boat anchor. He touched down fifteen or twenty feet below me and signaled like he wanted me to come to him. I did not move. My right leg was injured and very stiff. I could not put any weight on it. My chest was throbbing, and I had limited strength in my hands and arms due to the chest pain. My body was too beaten and bruised to try to stand up, let alone walk twenty feet down a seventy-degree slope.

He finally realized he was going to have to come get me, so he disconnected the hook from the cable, and used it like an ice axe to pull himself up to my position. It was difficult to hear and communicate with the noise of the helicopter overhead, but with hand signals and yelling I figured out what he wanted me to do. I asked him how we were going to get my gear up to the chopper. He responded, "Leave it!" I had just pulled it all out of the airplane and now it would be left in the snow, exposed to the elements. If I had known we were going to leave everything, I would have put my survival gear in the plane and left all my other valuables in the plane to protect them. He said we would be off in sixty seconds.

With the guardsman's "Leave it" ringing in my ears, I turned as quickly as the cold and the pain would allow and started throwing the stuff back in the plane. What didn't go in landed near the open cargo door, and I hoped it would be sheltered from the winter elements. I was also hoping that if anyone found the airplane and my belongings, they would first find some of the gospel tracts. Maybe some adventurer or wayward thief would be convicted, repent, ask God for forgiveness, and receive salvation. Maybe that is why I crashed.

The guardsman had me straddle two of the protrusions on the anchor-like contraption on which he had been lowered, and indicated that once he had it reattached to the cable, they would pull me up. Sounded like an adventure. Then, over the noise of the helicopter, he shouted that before they pulled me up, he would jump on.

"Jump on what?" I hollered.

"You!" he yelled. "It will hurt, but we'll be up in a moment."

He was right. It hurt.

On our way up to the helicopter, I got a view of the area and could see why they wanted to pull me up at the bottom of the slope instead of where I was sitting: the helicopter's blades were not that far from the rock ledge at the top of the ravine. One big wind gust would have made for some real trouble.

Once I was in the helicopter, everyone was all smiles and amazed at both my spirits and my apparently limited injuries. After a quick check of my vitals and some warm blankets, the helicopter turned toward Medford Airport and a waiting ambulance. I asked if I could look out the window to see where I was, so I rolled over to a small window and watched as my airplane and overnight sanctuary slipped out of view. I'm not sure how long it took to get to the Medford airport, maybe twenty-five to thirty minutes. As I listened to the whine of the helicopter rotors and gazed out the window, I was struck by the overwhelming love and grace of the Creator of the universe. There I was, being efficiently cared for by trained rescuers only a few hours after I should have been dead. The God who has the power and majesty to set the stars and planets in exacting orbits around the universe took the time to look after and protect me. I was in God's hands.

As we flew toward Medford, I learned the helicopter was out of Salem, Oregon, and they were running low on fuel. Hearing the words, "running low on fuel" certainly kept me from worrying about my gear. The hovering and waiting and burning of fuel above me before the actual rescue was due to their need to get specific permission from the forest service and government agencies to get close enough to the ground to initiate the rescue. I was in a protected national wilderness area and, although they had seen me alive and well on the ground, it seemed they still had to get specific approval to pick me up.

An ambulance was waiting at the edge of the tarmac off the runway, so once we landed the transfer was made very quickly and efficiently. The ambulance raced toward the Rogue Valley Medical Center with lights and sirens blaring. It was pretty exciting. The ambulance crew was amazed that I was in such great shape after crashing an airplane into the side of a mountain and then spending a freezing night in the open in the Cascade Mountains. Right away I let them know it was only through a miracle and the grace of God I was on that helicopter talking with them. All glory for my survival went to Him.

A Special Email

My son-in-law, Michael Collins, sent this email to about fifty friends and relatives a few days after the crash. He has some of the facts wrong, because he was relating only what he knew to be true at the time. This will give you a feel for what was running through the minds of my family members and loved ones soon after the crash.

Hi,

Some of you may or may not know by now that my wife Michelle's father crashed his single-engine plane on a dark, icy mountain peak ten nights ago on Friday, March 17ᵗʰ, in the snowy central Oregon Cascade Mountain Range. Miraculously, he is alive and well. Marshall was making a rushed flight from Klamath Falls to Eugene to be with his sister, who had just had a heart attack. He knew he was low on fuel and had gone through all the motions of flight preparation, but simply forgot to fuel his plane, even after rolling the fuel truck in place to fill up. It wasn't until he was almost to Eugene that it dawned on him that he hadn't fueled. He glanced at the fuel gauge, and it was already on 'empty.' He knew there was a Forest Service landing a ways behind him, so he turned around in an attempt to land there and to avoid populated areas. However, it was too late. Marshall was completely out of gas and began descending. He radioed Eugene to give his coordinates and asked the tower to tell his wife that he loved her and that he would see her in Heaven. At no point did Marshall expect to survive the crash or ask God to save him from the crash.

Around midnight, as the rugged mountains below the plane became more visible through the dark of night, and as he began to see trees underneath, Marshall slowed the plane as much as possible and prepared for impact. Ready for impact, Marshall found an icy patch as he passed over a ridge and immediately stalled the plane and shoved the yoke in to slam the nose of the plane down, in hopes of hitting the snow patch. He then grabbed the two pillows he had placed in the back seat of the plane (he was going to sleep on the floor at his sister's house) and placed them in front of his chest and his face. There was impact and he was in God's hands. He could feel glass and snow coming into the plane on his arms that were holding the pillows. The plane turned and then came to a rest. He was still alive!

Shortly after, pain began to fill Marshall's body. He felt he had broken an ankle and possibly some ribs. He was having trouble breathing. The nose of the plane was buried in the snow, so he punched out the back window of the plane with his hand, grabbed survival equipment (sleeping bag, flares, satellite phone, etc.), and was able to crawl out. When reaching back to grab one of the flares he had dropped, he felt something inside his chest snap back in to place and he was able to breathe properly again. His satellite phone had intermittent reception, but he was able to phone for rescue and call home. The ringer was off at home, but Michelle's mom just happened to get up at about 1 A.M. to go check the answering machine. Once she got the message, and after freaking out, she was able to coordinate with the search and rescue team to help get Marshall off the mountain. Many people prayed fervently as Marshall lay on his sleeping bag, not knowing what condition he was in. Marshall used flares to signal what he thought were rescue aircraft overhead at around 3 A.M. It wasn't until about 8 A.M. Saturday morning that a Black Hawk helicopter was able to lower a man on a rope to get Marshall out, because the terrain was too steep for a ground rescue. Although it seemed like an eternity for us, it was remarkably fast for a mountain rescue effort. He was airlifted to Medford and Michelle's mom drove over to meet him.

Miraculously, Marshall suffered "only" a broken ankle, a broken sternum, a bruised heart, and a bruised lung. Michelle drove up to assist in any way she could, along with my brother, Karston, and his wife Sarah. Marshall was discharged from the hospital the following Monday and is doing well at home now. He still has a lot of recovering to do, but is in good spirits. He still gets very emotional when he describes what happened that night, because he had no expectation of still being alive today. Our Lord Jesus still wants him here for a reason and what a powerful testimony he has. The FAA and Search & Rescue teams have already been in contact with Marshall to do some speaking regarding safety and survival.

I have attached some pictures taken by a pilot friend of Marshall and the Search and Rescue unit. In some images you have to zoom in to actually see the plane, but it gives you a good idea of the terrain he had to work with in the middle of the night. Anyway, I just wanted to share with you this miracle God has blessed our family with.

Michael

Final Thoughts From Cody

The morning after the crash

Mom told me my dad was going to be at Medford Hospital. My family and I went to see him as soon as we could. It was very hard for me to see him lying in the hospital bed all bruised and broken. I told him I planned on going up to the crash site the next day to retrieve some of his belongings. I went to about every sporting goods store in Medford, getting any maps of the area I could find. My sister, Heather, stayed at my parent's house to answer all of the phone calls that were coming in, and to help keep the house and kids in order. Russell, one of my dad's friends, heard that I wanted to go up and get his belongings out, and wanted to go with me. My best friend, Chris, and another friend of Dad's, Gordon, also went with me. We all got our packs and gear ready to leave the very next day.

Two days after the crash

Russell, Chris, Gordon, and I left Klamath Falls pretty early. We did not know what the weather forecast was or how we were going to get up the mountain. We decided to try to rent some snowmobiles and stopped at Diamond Lake resort. There were a couple guys there who heard what we were trying to do and offered to help by letting us use their snowmobiles to get to the top faster. Although once we got to the top, we would still need to hike a couple miles to the site of the crash. The trip was taking longer than we had planned and it was getting later and later. We decided we could not make it to the top that day. I was very disappointed; I really wanted to do this for my dad. I felt like I was not there for him when he really needed help getting off the mountain, and now I could not retrieve his belongings before they were lost to the weather. He was always there for me, and I wanted to be there for him, too.

CHAPTER 9

The Physical Recovery

"For I know the plans I have for you," declares the
Lord, "plans to prosper you and not to harm you,
plans to give you hope and a future."
(Jeremiah 29:11, NIV)

Judy

"How about I drive you to see Marshall right now,
Judy?" said the Sheriff's Deputy who was at the house and
kindly offered to drive me to Rogue Valley Medical Center
in Medford.

"No, I'll be all right, Sheriff. I really want to drive myself
and have a little bit of quiet time alone." It was one of those
times when I just needed to spend some quality time with
God to thank Him for saving my husband. Driving to the
hospital would be the perfect time to do that.

Rogue Valley Medical Center in Medford, Oregon, is
up and over the same mountains Marshall had crashed in,
and I can remember the drive as if it were yesterday. I drove

up the road and looked at the trees and all of the things God had created and I began thanking Him for protecting Marshall. I glanced up at the mountains and thought how Marshall had crashed and how unthinkable it was he had survived. The mountains are so steep and high, and I just remember thanking God and saying, "I can see it was your hand that protected him. Thank you, Lord, for sparing Marshall's life. I'm forever grateful to you." During those early morning hours, God and I had a good talk on the way to the hospital.

I did not know what to expect when I arrived. I pulled into the parking lot, got out of the car, and quickly walked inside. I was anxious to see Marshall, but concerned about what the damage to his body was going to look like.

The hospital staff directed me to his bed in the Emergency Room. When I walked through the doorway, our eyes met. He looked amazingly well. I walked over to him and gave him a big hug and a kiss, and he smiled. We both did. We talked quietly for a while, and he cried while he relayed the story to me. It was as if he was reliving every moment and experiencing all the feelings he had while gliding in the plane, knowing that God was with him.

Then the nurse came in and gave me his clothes—or what was left of them. They had to cut off his pants and T-shirt to see what sort of condition he was in and then start working on him. They brought the remnants of his clothing in to me in a bag. Everything was soaking wet. By that time, he had probably been in the hospital about two-and-a-half hours.

Later on that day, they brought me the shirt that Marshall had on when he left the house the evening of the crash. I took one look at it and started crying. God reveals His presence and talks to people in a multitude of ways. The Bible illustrates a few of these examples. He got Moses' attention though a burning bush; he spoke to Balaam through a donkey; he blinded Paul when he was converted. God makes His Word personal to each of us. This was my burning bush and the way God got my attention and revealed to me that He was in control. I knew I could totally rest in His sovereignty.

It was the strangest sight; Marshall's shirt was in perfect condition. He had crawled in and out of the plane *twice*, he had been lying in the snow for several hours, the emergency medical staff had cut his pants off, cut his T-shirt off, and yet the dress shirt he had been wearing throughout the whole ordeal didn't have *any* wrinkles on it. There was no blood on it, either. It was perfectly fine—clean and smooth. I almost did a double take.

"Did you guys do anything to this?" I asked the nurse.

"No, not at all Mrs. Alexander, we just took it off Marshall and hung it up," the nurse responded.

I cried some more.

It was God's personal way of reminding me that He had Marshall in the palm of His hand. I know that might sound silly to some people, but He was showing me through that shirt, He had been watching out for Marshall, and I could trust Him.

It did not take long for people to start showing up. Over the next few days as Marshall was recovering in the hospital, he had more visitors than I can count. It was like he was a rock star or a celebrity. Family members, friends from church, and folks from *The Way of the Master* training course Marshall had been teaching, all filled his room. Hospital staff from all departments came to see "the guy who survived a plane crash in the mountains." The doctors and nurses who came in and out of the room throughout his hospital stay said that Marshall must have had "angels on the mountain" with him. Others said, "You really have somebody watching out for you." The doctors, nurses, family, and friends comforted me in ways they will never know.

Everyone was expecting to see him in pieces, but that certainly wasn't the case—he was lying there on the bed telling them jokes. There were folks that came and wanted his autograph, too. I really laughed at that. So did Marshall. I think the medicine made him extra funny—he was entertaining everyone who stepped into the room.

It's our aim to bring God into everything that we do, and all of these things were open doors for Marshall to be able to recount the story of what happened and give *God* the glory.

Marshall

My chest was bruised badly. I could feel it. When I would try to move to a certain position, my chest would pop and pain would follow. To this day, I still have not swung a golf club. Any quick motions like that make me a little bit hesitant. My sternum was broken, but surprisingly, it was not painful. The impact of the crash also bruised my heart and right lung. For the first month or so, I could not roll over in bed or anything remotely like that, but soon after I healed very quickly. I know the entire recovery process was another miracle from God because it was surprisingly easy. The doctors were amazed.

I was in the hospital for only a few days and then was cleared to go home. Bed rest was what I needed most, and lots of it. The week before the accident, I had just finished remodeling a downstairs bedroom for guests. I had no way of knowing that I was actually remodeling that room for me, and that I would be the first "guest."

I was initially informed I had broken my right ankle. The doctor put a walking cast on me and told me to make an appointment with an orthopedist once I returned home to Klamath Falls. The doctor in Klamath Falls took five or six different X-rays of my ankle and foot, and then said:

"Mr. Alexander, I can see where there was a break on your foot, but I really don't see where you broke your ankle."

"Really?" I questioned.

"Yes," the doctor responded.

"Hmmmm, that's strange. When I was at Rouge Valley Hospital they said it was broken, but now you're saying it's not."

"That's correct, sir. The X-rays are clean."

I was pleasantly surprised and shocked at their diagnosis. I don't know if God healed my ankle or if it was misdiagnosed as broken, but I choose to give God the credit for it. After all, if He could save me from that mountain, He could certainly heal my ankle.

During my recovery, I had many hours to think about what I had just been through. I replayed the events just prior to the flight, my gliding to earth, the crash, and my rescue. I also could not help thinking about my next flying adventure, and, of course, what planes were out there to replace N6462A. Most of all, I was in prayer and study to seek God's direction for my family and me. He saved me from most certain death, so I had to make sure His love would be rewarded with my best efforts. I began to read God's Word a lot.

Now that I look back, it was sort of difficult to read. As I sat propped up in bed with the Bible on my lap, I really had to concentrate because the pain medication I was on affected my ability to concentrate.

I started with verses like:

> Beloved, think it not strange concerning the fiery trial which is to try you, as though some strange thing happened unto you: But rejoice, inasmuch as ye are partakers of Christ's sufferings; that, when his glory shall be revealed, ye may be glad also with exceeding joy. (1 Peter 4:12-13, KJV)

Then I was forced to stop and take a break because it was hard to focus my eyes. My body, including my eyes, had been through so many traumas. My experience was similar to people who have had a head-on collision in a car accident. The body goes through severe trauma upon impact: the heart gets pulled away from the muscles, the lungs bounce off the rib cage, and the retinas in the eyes can detach. The eyes are liquid, and all that force thrusts them forward, which was what happened to my eyes. It was one of the reasons the doctors felt my recovery would take so long.

But by God's grace, the only thing that really bothered me was my eyes. I started seeing little flashing white lights, especially at night. Apparently, both of my retinas were pulled away a bit in the crash, and what I was experiencing was the result. Nevertheless, I continued to plug away at reading the Bible and anything else inspirational that came to me:

> "Unless we deny ourselves and lay violent hands upon the impulses of our nature, we shall never come to the place where the crowns are distributed to the conquerors." (*Spurgeon Gold*, Ray Comfort, "The Daily Battle," pg. 36)

> *And he who searches our hearts knows the mind of the Spirit, because the Spirit intercedes for the saints in accordance with God's will. And we know that in **all things** God works for the good of those who love him, who have been called according to his purpose. For those God foreknew he also predestined to be conformed to the likeness of his Son, that he might be the firstborn among many brothers. And those he predestined, he also called; those he called, he also justified; those he justified, he also glorified. What, then, shall we say in response to this? **If God is for us, who can be against us?** (Romans 8:27-31, NIV, emphasis mine)

"For I know the plans I have for you," declares
the Lord, *"plans to prosper you and not to harm
you, plans to give you hope and a future."* (Jeremiah
29:11, NIV, emphasis mine)

Interestingly enough, the Jeremiah 29:11 passage was on
a banner I had hung up in the guest bedroom the very day
of the crash. I did not know that I had put it up specifically
to minister to myself.

Once I started feeling a little better, it was very hard
for me to sit and do nothing. The FAA, NTSB, and my
insurance company all were eager to know how the crash
happened and I wanted to get it all down on paper while it
was still fresh in my mind. I am not the fastest typist on the
block, but I can type somewhat decently. I would hobble to
my wife's computer until she would catch me and send me
back to bed. Then, I would hobble upstairs to my computer
until again I was caught. Judy was constantly shooing me
back to bed.

She would yell, "Marshall, you'd better rest yourself!"

"You're right," I'd say begrudgingly.

Then she would add, "You know that you should be
resting your body; that's the best thing for you, and that's
the doctor's orders."

"I know, but it's hard for me to just sit around in this
sick bed all day and all night," was my excuse.

However, she was right, and I would drag myself back
downstairs and into the bed. She was just looking out for
me, and I knew that, but if you're anything like me, it's hard
to stay in bed for several days at a time. I'm the type of

guy that has to be up and about doing things. Besides, this was a great opportunity to make my story into a testimony that these different agencies were *required* to read as part of their investigation. I was not about to miss this opportunity to share the gospel with them.

After typing up all the events of the crash and the miraculous things God did for me, I gave a copy to my pastor to read. When Pastor Jim and his wife were married fifteen years ago, her father was totally opposed to her marrying a preacher. It did not matter that Jim was an awesome guy; the fact that he was a preacher was all her dad needed to know when he decided to cut off almost all contact with them. Jim and his wife had been married about fifteen years when her dad decided to move to Europe. He came by their house to say goodbye and spend the night. Jim got up during the night and found his father-in-law reading my story. He looked up at Jim with tears in his eyes and asked,

"Do you know the guy in this story?"

Jim said, "Yes. He is a member of my church."

"So, do you really believe that what he wrote in here are his real feelings and are really true?" he asked.

Jim replied, "Oh, yes. I haven't read the story yet, but I know he is an honorable guy, loves the Lord, and is a good pilot."

"How could a guy really have faith like that?" he asked.

"Well, it's a gift of God. It's something that God has to work in your heart. Faith comes from having a personal relationship with Him," Jim explained. "You can have that much faith, too, if you turn to Christ. It's not just a feeling or an emotion: it is a reality when you know Him."

"Well, I never really thought about it that way," he said.

They stayed up until three in the morning talking about the things of God. It was an opportunity for Jim to talk to him like he never had before. His father-in-law did not move to Europe, and even though they are not sure if he became a Christian, he is willing to talk about it now.

I praise God when I hear about ways my story has impacted people's lives for the glory of God. If even one person gets saved, then everything I have been through has been worth it. Mark 16:15 says: *"Go ye into all the world, and preach the gospel to every creature."* And that is exactly what I intend to do.

CHAPTER 10

Good News

THOSE WHO KNOW YOUR NAME WILL TRUST IN YOU,
FOR YOU, LORD, HAVE NEVER FORSAKEN THOSE WHO
SEEK YOU." (PSALM 9:10, NIV)

August 2007

It's late August 2007, only five months after the crash. I'm older, feel more mature, definitely weigh more, and am out of shape compared to my younger, more active years. Injuries limited my physical activity the first few months after the crash, but earlier today I felt strong enough to take a day hike up the mountain. I'm planning to recover some of the few remaining items I was forced to leave behind the day I was rescued and also what I didn't recover during my trip back up here in June. Now, twelve hours into the "day" hike, it is night. The fact that I'm already on the ground and there is a very large and bright full moon are a couple of the big differences between this night and the one five months earlier.

The small headlamp on my ball cap visor gives just enough light to keep me from tripping over rocks, fallen trees, and changes in terrain, but not enough to see the trail ahead. When I hit a steep part of the trail, I notice how much heavier my pack is now that I've added the items I recovered at the crash site. I started the hike with around sixty pounds of supplies, including my satellite phone, which was recovered with the airplane a few months earlier. Yes, the same satellite phone that cost $65.00 a month and that people thought was a little extravagant. Five months earlier, up until the evening of March 16, 2007, I was beginning to think maybe they were right. Now I know that the satellite phone helped save my life.

Ironically, I'm frustrated with the phone right now because there's no reception. Without reception, I can't call my wife to let her know I'm fine and will be camping out overnight. I'm sure by this time she has worried herself sick, called all of the kids, and possibly even the sheriff and the search and rescue team.

Why am I back on this mountain and why do I feel it so important to return now? In part because I want to recover the remaining items from the crash, but mainly I just want to spend some time with God at the exact location He had chosen to spare my life. This spot on the mountain will always hold a special meaning for me, and it was summed up especially well in one of our local newspaper headlines that read:

Smashing Through Death's Door

Marshall Alexander died on March 16, 2007, when his plane crashed into the side of a mountain at night—Well, he should have died.

A New Plane

From almost day one after my rescue, I had been looking to find a new plane. At first, I could only look on the Internet, since I was confined to bed rest, but soon I was looking anytime I was out of the house. We went on a long, looping vacation that summer to Glacier National Park in Montana, Yellowstone National Park in Wyoming, Estes Park, and Rocky Mountain National Park in Colorado. I stopped at a few different airports along the way to look at the airplanes that were for sale. I had a great time test flying all the planes, but as I walked away from each plane, I did not feel a connection. My perseverance and patience finally paid off in Placerville, California, where I made a connection with a 1959 Cessna 182, three years younger than my original 1956 Cessna, but basically the same plane. It was obvious the owner had taken great care of this plane—it was immaculate. What I liked best about it were the avionics and the same straight tail as the 1956 version. I had found the newest member of my "fleet."

Before the crash, I would fly almost weekly, either for fun or to take a friend where they needed to go. Sometimes I would tell Judy, "Honey, I need to get away from the house. I'm going to go to the airport," and then I'd go up in the air by myself to do touch-and-goes or just to look at the scenery. To me, flying is a stress reliever. To be up in the heavenlies, flying and moving the plane around any way I wanted. Such freedom.

Unfortunately, these days—with the economy going sour—I've hardly flown at all. It's just too expensive, and my own personal finances have deteriorated quite a bit. Flying is not a priority and is low on the budget list.

Airplane fuel has been up to $4.50 to $5.00 a gallon. A two-hour, fun-flight can cost up to $180. Nowadays I have to budget carefully and save before I can justify going up just to look at the scenery.

After the crash, I was apprehensive about night flying. Flying in the dark is quite different from daytime flight; anything can happen, and your options are limited. The parts of the country where I fly are not flat like Texas, where you can probably land a plane almost anyplace, even at night. Where I fly, it is mountainous, with very limited space for safe emergency landings—day or night. I learned first hand that there are not many options at night. The few times I did fly at night after the crash, I was apprehensive and my palms got a bit sweaty. Even though the crash was a result of my own pilot error, all the memories of the crash were swirling in my head.

A Few Important Questions

You have been reading my miracle story. Crash landing an airplane in the rugged Cascade Mountains with minimal injury in any scenario is miraculous, but at night, in the winter, and with no light from the moon, it is truly a miracle. My head was covered and my eyes were closed. Where I crash-landed the airplane was the result of a higher power.

I hope it has made you think about your own eternal destiny. I hope the telling of this miracle has helped you to realize there truly is a God, the same God of yesterday, today, and tomorrow. He is the King of kings, and Lord of lords—the King who created the universe and lovingly created you and me. He is the same kind, gentle, and loving

God that plucked me out of the sky and set my airplane down in a soft snowfield.

Now I need to ask you a few very important questions. Have you come to the place in your spiritual life where you know for certain, were you to die today, that you would go to Heaven? Or is that something you're still thinking about? The Bible was written for you, so you might know without a doubt if you will go to Heaven or hell.

I'd like to ask you another question: If you were to die today, and were standing before God, and He asked, "Why should I let you in my Heaven?" how would you answer? Your answer today will be the determining factor of your eternal destiny. This isn't a trick question, but there is only one correct answer. Listen to your God-given conscience. Speak to God with an honest heart.

Have you ever lied?

Have you ever stolen anything?

Have you used God's name as a curse word?

Have you violated *any* of the other Ten Commandments? (See Exodus 20.)

The Bible says we die once, and then we are judged by God. If we break even one of His Laws, we are condemned to hell. After evaluating your life against God's Law, the Ten Commandments, do you think you'll go to Heaven or hell?

The good news is the Bible says, *"God demonstrates His own love toward us, in that while we were still sinners, Christ died for us"* (Romans 5:8, NKJV). Jesus suffered and died on the Cross, bearing the punishment for your sins. Then He rose from the dead, thereby defeating death. If you repent—that is, turn away from your sins—and trust in the Savior, God will forgive you and grant you eternal life. Jesus said, *"Unless one is born again, he cannot see the kingdom of God"* (John 3:3, NASB). If you are not born again, you cannot enter Heaven. Right now, or tonight before you go to bed, talk to God—that's what prayer is. Prayer is simply a two-way conversation between your Creator and Redeemer, and you.

Pray something like this:

Dear God,

I confess I am a sinner. Thank you that Jesus took my punishment upon himself when he died on the Cross for my sins. Thank you that he rose from the dead, defeating death—for me. Today, I repent of my sins and place my trust for my salvation in Jesus Christ.

In Jesus' name, Amen.

Read the Gospel of John in the Bible, especially John 14:12. Then, read your Bible daily and obey what you read. Find a Christ-centered, Bible-based church to attend and ask the pastors any questions you might have. I personally pray that when God has called both of us to eternity, I will see you in Heaven with me.

CHAPTER 11

Life Today

To everything there is a season,
a time for every purpose under heaven:
A time to be born, and a time to die....
(Ecclesiastes 3:1-2, nkjv)

I teach the "Truth Project" class at church on Tuesday nights, as well as working *The Way of the Master* booth at the Klamath County Fair and other local county fairs and events. Today is the first day in three weeks that nothing is going on other than church tonight. Satan has been trying to discourage Judy and me from continuing on in our ministry and witnessing, telling us that our efforts are a waste. But I am reminded that nowhere in the Bible does God judge us on success. It is merely our job to share the gospel and it's God's job to convict the hearts of the people we talk to. So, I continue to teach my class and work at the county fairs, even when my enthusiasm is not what it should be.

It is obvious to me that we are in a spiritual battle. Just the other night, I was out in the barn praying and seeking

God during a spiritual storm, as well as during an actual thunderstorm. I was talking things out with God when I heard an explosive boom of thunder. The whole barn shook! I stepped outside and looked at the sky. Right over our property was a big, black, angry-looking thundercloud. That huge, black cloud was moving and swirling fiercely as if it were about to unleash its fury on us. Astonishingly, right next to it was a big, beautiful rainbow. What an amazing sight! The rainbow was a reminder of God's faithfulness to His people even in the midst of the fury of the storm. I was reminded that with God, there is always hope and I had to stay faithful to Him.

The floodgates of hell continue to try to destroy individuals, families, and faith. From that first lie of Satan in the Garden of Eden up to the present, he continues to try to destroy us through the lies he subtly weaves into our lives and our culture.

I wrote portions of this story within weeks of my airplane crash. Other parts, I have written over time since the crash, and now I am writing these words two years after the accident. For me, life's challenges continue—as does the battle for people's salvation.

I am reminded of an exchange between two characters in a film we recently watched. "Have you lived your whole life here?" the one character asked. The other's response was, "Well, not yet!"

The Story Continues

So, does anything happen after the crash? Is this the end of the crash story? Does everyone live happily ever after? Has God's plan for my life been fulfilled? What else is there?

Well, the story of the Alexander family continues, as do the challenges to our faith. But God is faithful and He will win in the end. My God-given iron will, with *His* help will prevail.

For the past thirteen years, when someone would ask, "Do you have any children?" I would respond, "We have a few—eight." Of those eight children, five have been adopted, and three of those were through Oregon's children's services. My wife and I were foster parents for several years and a few of those children just never went home, so we adopted them. From my own experience as a foster child for six years, and my wife's childhood experiences, we thought that God had called us to help children who were having challenges in their homes and needed a safe environment in which to live. If my memory is correct, over several years we have had twenty-two children live with us from a few days to a few months to a few years. When our younger children make bad decisions, Judy can't sleep. She'll stay up during the night and pray. She takes great comfort in God's Word in these moments.

Journal Entries

September 21, 2009

I am up in Washington State visiting my parents. Neither one is in good health. Today I am in Bellingham visiting my dad for four days, and then I'll be in Tri-Cities visiting my mom. I flew up in the Cessna.

My dad will not be on this Earth much longer. I thought we were going to lose him Saturday night, but as of this morning, he was holding his own and doing better. He knows his time is short, so we had some good conversations. I prayed and talked with him about his eternal destiny. I believe he repented and turned from his sin and turned to God. I now know that his future is in God's hands and his salvation and forgiveness are from Jesus alone. Dad asked me for my forgiveness for many of the things he'd done, and for some things he didn't do, while I was growing up. I figure if Dad is asking me for forgiveness now, it's only because he asked Christ's forgiveness first. I have much more confidence I will see him in Heaven. After forty-plus years of uncertainty, that is great news.

September 30, 2009: 3:30 P.M.

We continue having a hard time with one of our children. Things do not seem to be going well.

September 30, 2009: 7:30 P.M.

I just received a call from one of my brothers in Washington State. My youngest sister, Suanne, just died of a heart attack at the age of forty-two. Suanne was my half-sister, born during my mother's second marriage. She had not been feeling well for the past week and went to the emergency room. The hospital staff was running tests in order to diagnose her condition when she had a heart attack. They were unable to revive her. She left behind her husband and two children.

I may be leaving tonight to go north again to comfort my mom and stepfather. Suanne and my mom were best friends, so Mom will have a hard time. Suanne was a great mom and knew the Lord, so we know she is more alive now than we are. God has taken her home and given her a new body. I thank God for this and for her salvation.

September 30, 2009: 10:00 P.M.

I just received a call from my stepmother indicating that my dad has turned for the worse and they have put him on a morphine drip. He is unconscious, and she is uncertain how long he will last. I told her I am heading up to Washington in the morning to go to the Tri-Cities because my sister just died. I will keep in touch and come over to see my dad if I can work it out.

October 2, 2009: 10:30 P.M.

I got a phone call that Dad just died. From my dad's last conversations, I am hopeful that he is now with Jesus and has a new body and has no more pain and suffering.

Monday, December 07, 2009: 1:09 P.M.

Mom's passing on December 5, and my announcement to family and friends:

Dear friends and relatives,

Many of you know that my mom, Stella, has been battling type-4 leukemia for the past eight years. A year-and-a-half earlier she had been diagnosed with breast cancer and underwent surgery and months of radiation treatment. Then came the leukemia and years of chemotherapy. At the time of her last diagnosis, they gave her five years to live. She lived eight more years. Two years ago, she again faced breast cancer and had a total mastectomy of one breast. The operations were successful and once again she beat the odds. After multiple blood transfusions due to the leukemia, she had her spleen removed. Unfortunately, she contracted MRSA and had to endure several hospitalizations. Recently, the leukemia was taking its toll and medical options were depleted. Mom was dying. We brought her to Springfield, Oregon, to my sister Debby's house— to die. We thought it might be a few weeks, but it was only a few days.

Stella went to be with the Lord Saturday, December 5, 2009, at 6:37 A.M. in the morning. My sisters Starlene, Debby, and Danette, and brother Greg and I were at her side. I spent the night thinking she may not make it through the night, and I did not want to be sleeping and not be there with her. I was rubbing her arm and her back as she took her last shallow breath—and she was gone. With tears of sadness and tears of joy for Mom's homecoming, all of us prayed and sang with the realization that our mother was now at the feet of Jesus and her battles were over. She was now with our youngest sister, Suanne, who had preceded her in death by only a few months. What a reunion it must have been!

Marshall J. Alexander

Monday December 14, 2009: 11:00 A.M.

I spoke at my mom's funeral:

My mom, Stella Ann, was not perfect, just as none of us is perfect. Despite imperfection, she left behind a legacy of courage, perseverance, and faith for the future.

Stella was a great wife, mother, grandmother, great-grandmother, and friend to many.

In all of these roles, she was also a great teacher. She loved to teach—especially when children were around. She would not just play with them and entertain them; she would use her creative skills and childlike spirit to teach them. This is where the legacy starts. She would teach them about God, and the famous men and women of the past who significantly affect us today. She loved to teach about our Founding Fathers and the roots of America, and often she would just teach trivia and facts: What is the longest river, highest waterfall, tallest mountain? Many in this room, many who are now adults, were befriended by Stella and once sat at her teacher's feet. How many can attest to that? Look around. You are looking at her legacy.

Her legacy as a teacher and mentor lives on with many of you in this room. My mom was a teacher to the end. In fact, she taught me a valuable lesson with her last breath.

I want to talk about my mom's final lesson—the lesson she taught me as she took her final breath at 6:37 A.M., last Saturday, December 5.

But let me digress for a minute. As God would have it, my dad, Alex, [Bill] Stella's first husband, also died recently, only two months earlier, on October 2. The phrase "last breath" had great significance during his last days also.

The greatest and most important lessons I learned from Mom and Dad at a very young age were the lessons and truth about God's saving grace and God's amazing sacrifice of His Son Jesus for our sins. Unfortunately, after those early lessons, my dad turned from Christ, and for the next fifty years rejected the Bible's teaching and embraced the love of the flesh and the world—which was an indication that earlier he had been a false convert.

In the end, my dad was battling lung cancer and even with his knowing that his time was short, rejected my attempts to talk about salvation in Jesus. So I gave up on him. I had determined there was nothing else for me to do except pray, even though I did not think that would help after all these years. I did not even go to see him for eighteen months—until recently.

However, one day in prayer, I distinctly had the impression from God that there was still hope, until Dad took his last breath. That phrase "hope until his last breath" stuck with me and convicted me that I needed to keep praying and talking to my dad until his last breath. As a result, I did go see him again a couple of times over the last few months, and during his last few days on this Earth. God the Holy Spirit had been working on him. He was attached to an oxygen machine with a twenty-five-foot hose and he was sitting in front of the television, which, during all of the time I was visiting, was either broadcasting Fox News or the Christian channel. Despite my dad's worldly and liberal attitudes over the last fifty years, he was now engrossed in the Tea Parties, Glenn Beck, Sean Hannity, and Christian programming.

I am confident God's work was done in my dad's final days, and I can hope for his eternal salvation. Last Saturday, December 5, my mom Stella had a reunion with her mom and dad, her brother and sisters, my dad Alex, and her youngest daughter, my sister, Suanne. They were all in Heaven because they all repented and turned from their sins and trusted in Jesus Christ to save them.

But let me get back to Mom's final lesson. In memory of her, I wrote a letter, which reads:

Dearest Mother,

I wanted to write you this final letter of thanks, as a tribute to your courage and strength as a loving mother and teacher. I now know you were teaching me yet another very valuable lesson with your last breath.

As you know, all of us kids spent most of Friday night with you. You were no longer responding to us, but I think you could still hear us talking, singing, and praying as you continually breathed deeply. As the evening progressed, hour after hour, you struggled to take your next breath, with a long pause of relaxation before you breathed again. I hope you heard all of us, as it was a time of rejoicing for your life, Mom. All of us kids prayed, worshiped, cried, and laughed throughout the night as we reflected on your wonderful legacy. During the night, each of us made various pledges to ourselves and to each other of specific ways we would adopt or continue activities that you promoted. We pledged to continue them as a tribute to you.

None of us has been getting much sleep of late, so we decided to take shifts to be with you. As Friday evening turned to early Saturday morning, Starlene and I were the only ones at your bedside. For hours, I sat next to you, rubbing your arm and rubbing your back as you just lay there and breathed. Starlene and I prayed God would take you home so that your struggles would be over. What was left to be done? We told you we loved you. You had done your work on this Earth well, and it was okay to go home to the Lord. I was asking God, "What else is there to do?" It did not appear that you were in any pain, but I know you were struggling to take each breath. Why struggle, why keep fighting, Mom? You and God knew what you were doing. You were teaching me another lesson.

Starlene and I talked throughout the night and we would pause and wonder what Mother was waiting for, or if it was the Lord providing more time for us to complete something with you, with each other, or with Him. Although we had marvelous times of worship and prayer, it was a mystery why you were still fighting so hard. Each breath was labored and deep as you sort of held your breath for up to twenty seconds until the next breath. Why were you so determined to keep breathing? Why was God allowing you to keep breathing, rather than taking you home? As I was holding your hand

and witnessing this demonstration of courage and resolve, I, too, had the resolve that I must keep fighting for each breath and each moment. Life is precious. I can't give up. I was thinking about your example. You would not give up; you would keep breathing and fighting to the end. We gave you permission to leave, but you didn't. You kept struggling to breathe.

I mentioned to Star about my new resolve to not give in or give up. I need to keep breathing and fighting and running the race for Christ. Star asked if I had been losing hope and giving up. I indicated I had had some deep struggles lately, with finances, our children, direction for our lives, etc. Star talked to me about David, how during much of his life he was crying out to God, because things were hard, and yet he ended his psalms with affirmation of the grace and mercy of God in his life. It's always about total abandonment to God.

Starlene came around to my side of your bed, Mom, and prayed with me. She prayed for God's presence to be personal and present in my life, and that the reality that our loving heavenly Father wants and ordains only the very best for our lives, even through pain and struggle, and would be ever present with us (see Romans 8:28). She also shared the statement, which is the summary of Ephesians, "It is true we must walk among men, and it is true that we must stand against the wiles of the devil, but we dare not walk, and we dare not stand, until we have sat well at His feet." We must learn to trust in the goodness of the Lord, learning to enjoy His presence and resting in His sovereignty, knowing that He is in control of all things for His good pleasure and our own good.

Star finished praying and shared what she heard on a CD she had been listening to: We should consider Abraham. God had made him a promise, and yet for much of his life he lived through events that called into question God's ability and willingness to fulfill His Word. And then, after many years, God did fulfill His Word with the birth of Isaac. Then, of all things, God asked Abraham to take the only token of His promise—Isaac—and place him on an altar to be killed. Thus, the apparent promise would come to an end. Was Abraham confused, anxious, and doubtful? It just didn't make any sense to kill the very thing that would fulfill God's promise to him.

Thus, the reality is, we have to trust Him—even when we cannot make sense of things.

I told Star, in jest, that it was not really a very hard decision for Abraham to consider killing Isaac, because Isaac was a teenager.

We both laughed at my joke. And you, Mom, took your last breath and were called up to Heaven.

Starlene and I looked at each other with tears in our eyes, as we now knew what you were waiting for. You were waiting to teach me this lesson: "Keep fighting, keep breathing, and keep laughing, until your last breath. With God all things are possible."

Thanks, Mom, for this reminder and this final lesson. I now know that your final struggling breaths were for me, to teach me this very important lesson. I will not forget it until my own final breath.

Love, Your son, Marshall

This was a very personal lesson from my mother. However, we all live in hard times. With the poor economy, the state of the world, and many uncertainties, others in this room may also have seemingly insurmountable struggles. God does not promise us a life without struggles, but He does promise He will be with us through those struggles. This lesson and reminder from Stella was directed at me, but it is a life lesson for all of us. Stella is in Heaven, but I know she wants us all to trust in God, through Jesus Christ, and keep fighting for what is right and good in the Lord's eyes, no matter what.

Ten out of ten people die—they just don't know when it will happen. In fact, it is estimated that between 150,000 and 180,000 people die each day around the world. Most all of them wake up in the morning, not realizing that this is the very day they will take their last breath. I hope many are prepared for that event, but I know many are not.

What does it mean to be prepared for your final breath? The Bible says that when we take that final breath and pass to the other side, we will face judgment. Hebrews 9:27, NIV says: *"Just as man is destined to die once, and after that to face judgment."* That judgment will either send us to Heaven or send us to hell. Romans 5:8, NIV states the good news: *"But God demonstrates his own love for us in this: While we were still sinners, Christ died for us."*

Man is inherently evil; we are sinners and we need to be redeemed—saved—from that sin. If I tell a lie, I have sinned, and I am a sinner. If I steal, no matter the value of the object, time, or idea, I'm a sinner. If I lust, I sin. We are not able to redeem, or save, ourselves from the judgment we deserve. Only faith in Jesus Christ can accomplish that miracle. The solution is simple, yet profound: You must understand that you are a sinner, that your sins are crimes against God, repent of those sins, ask Jesus to forgive you, and receive Him as your Lord and Savior from this day forward.

If you are a relative or were a friend of Stella Ann, I know she wants to see you in Heaven with her when you pass from this Earth. But more importantly, God is pleading for you, through me, to turn from your sin and turn to Him—and then you *will* pass from death to eternal life through His Son, Jesus Christ.

While we were going through my mom's things, we came upon a Bible that I had given to her for Christmas over twenty years ago. In the front of the Bible, Mom had taped a poem. Above it, she wrote: "Thank you, Jesus. November 9, 1995, 6:10 P.M."

I am not sure what struggles she was going through that evening in 1995, but this poem must have strengthened her during that season of her life:

Faith Is Stronger Than My Fears

Sometimes my cross is hard to bear
for there is darkness everywhere,
and troubles pile around my door,
like autumn leaves forevermore.

The morning light seems far away,
like I am stuck in yesterday.
My heart is beating like a drum—
I try to pray, but words won't come.

But then the sun begins to rise
and hope is born within my eyes.
A rainbow forms among my tears
for faith is stronger than my fears!

by Clay Harrison

I SOUGHT THE LORD, AND HE HEARD ME,
AND DELIVERED ME FROM ALL MY FEARS.
(PSALM 34:4, NKJV)

CHAPTER 12

Questions and Answers

DEAR FRIENDS, DO NOT BE SURPRISED AT THE PAINFUL TRIAL
YOU ARE SUFFERING, AS THOUGH SOMETHING STRANGE WERE
HAPPENING TO YOU. BUT REJOICE THAT YOU PARTICIPATE IN
THE SUFFERINGS OF CHRIST, SO THAT YOU MAY BE OVERJOYED
WHEN HIS GLORY IS REVEALED. IF YOU ARE INSULTED BECAUSE
OF THE NAME OF CHRIST, YOU ARE BLESSED, FOR THE SPIRIT
OF GLORY AND OF GOD RESTS ON YOU. IF YOU SUFFER, IT
SHOULD NOT BE AS A MURDERER OR THIEF OR ANY OTHER
KIND OF CRIMINAL, OR EVEN AS A MEDDLER. HOWEVER, IF
YOU SUFFER AS A CHRISTIAN, DO NOT BE ASHAMED, BUT
PRAISE GOD THAT YOU BEAR THAT NAME.
(1 PETER 4:12-16, NIV)

Q: Do you think you'll ever forget to fuel up again before takeoff?

Nope, never! I think I have learned my lesson. Besides, no one will ever let me forget!

Q: How was it possible that you forgot to fuel up even after going through your check list?

Once you're on the ramp and you do your scan of the panel, you see all your flight instruments and the oil pressure, carb heat, vacuum, etc. You see every needed gauge except the fuel gauges. A 1956 Cessna 182 is a high wing—wings on top of the plane—with the fuel gauges up in the ceiling, slightly behind the pilot's view. You have to specifically lean back and look up behind you to see the gauges. At night, I would have to get the flashlight out and shine it up behind me to see the gauges, which I normally don't do because I would have fueled the plane anyway.

Newer planes have fuel gauges built into the panel similar to automobile fuel gauges, but the Cessna's were float gauges. They are not very accurate unless there is slight movement, but if there is too much movement, they jump around a lot and you can't read them, so they are not accurate while the plane is sitting on the ground. The most accurate way to check for fuel is to climb up to the fuel-filing ports and dip the tanks—put a stick in the tank and see how much fuel is in there.

Normally, I just fuel up and top off the tank at every opportunity to make sure I have fuel. That was my intent the evening of the crash—to top off the tanks so that I would not need to look at the gauges or dip the tanks.

I don't always take my truck with the fuel tank to the airport because the truck itself is old and tends to be a gas hog. I only take it when I plan on fueling the airplane. I knew I needed to fuel up, but when I got there, I spaced out. That was the problem. The cause of the crash was that I simply didn't fuel up.

My flight preparation is also much different on my plane when it is stored in my own hanger between uses. When I rented planes to fly, everything including fuel was always an issue because you had no idea who or how the airplane had been flown last, so you had to be sure. I know that when my airplane is locked up in the hanger, no one else has touched it, flown it, or used my fuel.

The bottom line is that if I had done everything correctly, I would not be writing this story. I would have fueled up and made one more flight just like the other hundreds I had made before. That is why it is called an accident. But I know that there are no accidents in God's scheme of things. I thank Him for saving me from the crash and allowing me to live another day. And perhaps He has used this story to touch just one life. It would have been worth it all if just one person repents and trusts in Jesus Christ.

Q: Can you tell us more about your ankle that was broken, and then was not?

My ankle was completely swollen and I could not walk on it. The doctor said that I had done a lot of damage to it. I was told that I should not be walking on it or doing anything on it for a whole year. However, within two to three months, I was walking on it and doing fine.

The doctor said it would take anywhere from a year to two years before my sternum would be healed, and that I should not drive. My wife and I have a motor home, and we went on a trip six weeks after the crash, and guess who drove the motor home? My blood pressure is really low, and my heart rate is low as well, and those are two things that promote healing. I just naturally heal fast, even though I am an old man of fifty-eight years.

Five months later, I was well enough to hike up the Cascade Mountains to where I crashed my plane—with a sixty-pound pack on my back.

Judy and I went on a trip to Israel with our church that October. I walked all over the place and was fine.

The doctors have no explanation for my foot healing so fast. But of course, I do: God healed it.

Q: Have you been able to share your story with others?

Lots of people have heard and been affected by the story. What is interesting is that when I was looking for airplanes around the country and emailing sellers, I would always send them a note with a copy of the email version of the story. The note said:

> Dear Sirs:
>
> I am looking for a new airplane because I crashed my plane and survived. I have attached my story. When you get a free moment, please take the time to look over it. Thank you and take care.

As a result, I would sometimes get a response telling me about a close encounter they had while flying. Others would email and say, "Thanks for the story," or "Your story really had an impact on me."

I have never heard of anyone saying they got saved or turned to Christ because of my story, but I leave the saving up to the Lord. I planted the seeds; He will give the increase.

I use my story when I am out on the streets witnessing, or when we set up a *The Way of the Master* evangelism booth. I have made a lot of photocopies of the story. I laminated one copy and pinned it up on one of the booth posts. When people walk by the booth see it flapping in the wind, they pause and walk closer to it. It opens the door to share the gospel. "Do any of those pictures look familiar?" I ask. And they say, "Yes. Oh, is that *you*?" I tell them it is and they want to hear more.

The big daily paper in town, which is sent out to residents, is called *The Herald and News*. They called me wanting to cover the story.

"Mr. Alexander, we heard about your plane crash and how you survived, and we would like to hear about the details of what exactly happened to you," they said.

"That would be great, and you might be happy to know that I have already written a story and I can email it to you if you would like," I said.

"Sure that would be fine, Mr. Alexander."

"Oh, and one more thing, if you are going to cover the story, I want to make sure that you include the portions that I wrote about God. It is important to me that I am not seen as the hero in this story, but that *God* is. I want to give Him the praise and honor for what happened to me."

"Okay, Mr. Alexander, well, thank you," they said.

I never heard back from them. But God had other things in store.

Another local newspaper called *The Pioneer Press* contacted me, and I emailed my story to them. About an hour later, I heard back from them.

"Mr. Alexander, my name is Lance and I am a staff writer for *The Pioneer Press*. I just read your story, and I have got to come over. Can I come over and talk to you?"

"Sure, Lance, that would be just fine."

"Your story is amazing. I have got to talk to you right now about it, and I don't want to put it off. I'll be right over," Lance said.

Lance came over with the owner of the newspaper. After I spent some time relaying all that had happened, they were really impressed. The newspaper owner said, "I would really like to run this story as a special edition just before Easter, and it is such a compelling story, could you write a salvation message at the end of it for me?"

I was floored—*The Pioneer Press* is a secular newspaper. The other paper did not want anything to do with me, and this one was asking me to include a salvation message at the end. What a blessing!

On Wednesday, April 4, I was featured on the front page of *The Pioneer Press*.

The great thing about all of this is that Lance had grown up in church, but was not following the Lord. The story ended up being a witness to him and for him. It confronted some of the issues in his life. He was really interested in it. Two weeks after the story ran, he was in a near-fatal car wreck. He hit a curb, flipped his car, and ended up in a ditch. He was messed up a lot more than I was after my airplane crash.

He was on life support for a couple of weeks, then in a coma. His mother called me—she is a believer—and asked if I would come up to the hospital and pray for him. Off and on, I went to the hospital and prayed with her and for him. Eventually, he came out of the coma and started recovering.

I do not have a lot of contact with him now, but the story goes on.

At the Klamath County Fair, his son came to *The Way of the Master* evangelism booth that we set up. I was going through the normal *The Way of the Master* material with him and witnessing to him—showing him gospel tracts and presenting the whole thing—and he said, "Well, I know you."

"You do?"

"Yes."

"You know my dad."

"Really?" I questioned.

"My dad is the one who wrote that article in the paper—he wrote about you and your plane crash."

"Oh! Yes, well, how are you and he doing?" I inquired.

"Well, my dad is doing well. He is still struggling though, but I know that writing that article about you and then praying with you has helped a lot," he said.

I was glad to hear he was doing better.

As a result of publishing the article on me, the owner of *The Pioneer Press* said that he got many new subscription requests with letters saying that they were proud of him for publishing my story with a gospel message. That was the first time he had ever gotten notes from readers or that many new subscribers.

On the flip side, *The Herald and News* was never heard from again.

I also had my story published in the May-June 2007 copy of the *Civil Air Patrol* magazine. It was titled "Angels Above." This was another wonderful opportunity for God to be magnified through the crash story in a nationally circulated magazine.

Here are the opening lines of the story published in the magazine:

> On any other day, the drone of a passing plane's prop might seem ordinary. Not for Marshall Alexander. Shortly after 10 P.M. on a starry March night, Alexander crash-landed his 1956 Cessna 182 in the snowy, steep Cascade Mountains of southwest Oregon. His bones were broken, his body was spent, and he was all alone. Twice the sound of propellers caused his heart to jump with relief as planes hummed overhead, but the aircraft kept flying toward Portland, oblivious of the needy aviator. Alexander *prayed to God for help, and his prayers were answered.*

Q: Can you remember any of the other songs you sang on the mountain when you were waiting to be rescued?

Looking back, I can recall some of the songs, but it is hard to remember them all. One of the songs people do not sing much anymore, but I sing to myself all the time (and I do not even know the name of), goes:

> *He's the King of kings, He's the great I Am, He's the Bright and Morning Star; He's the Prince of Peace, He's the Way, the Truth, and Life, and He's mine, oh, yes, He's mine. He is my Savior, He is my God, He is my shelter in the time of storm; He's the Alpha and Omega, the Beginning and the End, and He's mine, oh, yes, He's mine.*

I never hear anybody sing that song anymore, so I do not even know where it came from. He is the shelter in the storm, He's the rock—you know all those images were a comfort when I was struggling on the mountain.

Q: *What helps you cope with the different storms and trials in your life?*

Since the crash, life definitely has not been easy. Judy and I keep saying, "It sure would be nice to have a week in our life that is not filled with trials. Would that not be amazing?" Sometimes I start to feel sorry for myself, thinking that it is not fair that I have so many trials.

But whenever I pray, "Lord, please give us a break," I immediately think of a book that I have by DC Talk called *Jesus Freaks*. It is an amazing book filled with story after story about martyrs and how they never denied Christ, even in the midst of unthinkable torture and persecution. After reading about the horrendous things these people have gone through, I immediately stop feeling sorry for myself.

139

All of us can have tough times in our lives, and we can go through unbearable things. But when I pick up *Jesus Freaks* and read about precious saints being beaten in ways that are horrifying, or of men forced to watch their wives being raped and their children killed in front of their eyes, it helps me continue to press on and live for the Lord. It is an amazing book to remind you of what is important, to see what other people endure for Jesus' name, and how they still do not deny Him, but praise Him. Sadly, these horrendous things are still happening today, all around the world.

When you are going through something difficult yourself, it is not easy, but reading a book about those who are tortured and die for Christ helps me put things in perspective. I can't say I am still overjoyed by all the trials that come my way, but a book like this gives me perspective: What I am going through is not anything compared to what some people endure for Jesus' name. After all, the Bible tells me, *"I can do all things through Him who strengthens me"* (Philippians 4:13, NASB). The context of this verse is clear: when God calls me to endure, He supplies the grace to do so; through the grace of God, I can overcome every trial and temptation that comes my way.

Q: *Did you ever find the perfect role model that you were looking for as a young boy?*

Yes. His name is Jesus Christ. As I've grown in my Christian walk, I've come to realize that everyone and everything will let you down. Family members will fail you, church members will hurt you, things grow old, people grow old and die. Jesus Christ is the only one who is the same yesterday, today, and forever. He doesn't grow old, won't let you down, and will not leave you or forsake you. He is the perfect role model.

Q: How did you learn of Ray Comfort and Kirk Cameron and their ministry, **The Way of the Master?**

I saw their program on the Trinity Broadcasting Network (TBN). I thought their teaching on evangelism was so good I immediately called the ministry and ordered the entire first season of the television program. I watched the whole thing as soon as it arrived in the mail.

The Way of the Master opened my eyes to the fact that not everyone that goes *to* church is *of* the Church. I mean, I knew in my heart that half the people who are in church are not really Christians, but the program made it clear to me why that was the case. If the folks in church are really saved, then why do they do the things they do? And why do they not share their faith and have a passion to serve in the local church? I had always known in my heart of hearts that everyone sitting in church could not possibly be saved, yet hearing Ray Comfort's message, "True and False Conversion," was like "Whoa! That is what it is!" It finally all made sense to me. They have a terrific website *www.wayofthemaster.com* with many helps for witnessing and for a faithful Christian life. Make sure when you visit the website that you listen to the free message, "True and False Conversion."

Dr. D. James Kennedy, at his "Evangelism Explosion" seminars, said that from his own empirical data probably only 10 percent of the people in church are true Christians and will make it to Heaven. I thought this was terribly sad.

Growing up in and attending Assembly of God churches, Four Square churches, and Open Bible churches for most of my adult life, I've found they are all more evangelical than many other denominations. The downside is they are more emotional. So, when a lot of these "Christians" would become emotional, raise their hands, praise the Lord and jump up and down, and then go out and have an affair the next day, I began to wonder—really wonder—about their salvation. Ray's message made everything crystal clear for me.

Even in church now, when I see all this emotion and people getting excited, I think, "I want to see the *fruit*—I do not want to see the *emotion*. I want to know what you do outside of church, when nobody is watching." It is obvious how few in the pews are truly saved when I host *The Way of the Master* training at church or when we try to hit the streets to share our faith: it is hard to recruit people—to find people who want to participate. The people who do go out to witness just love it. They are always asking, "When are we going to go share our faith?" and "When are we going to go out again?" or "Do you know when the next fair is going to be?" We should not have to coerce people to share their faith. You know what I mean? After all, it's commanded in the Bible. Christians should *want* to share their faith.

Folks need to hear the Law of God (the Ten Commandments) and see their sin before they can understand their need for the Savior. Many individuals today hear, "Jesus loves you and has a wonderful plan for your life," and they want that wonderful plan and that love. But when the trials of life come in—they are diagnosed with cancer, or they lose their life savings—they fall away from Christ. This is because they were never of Him; they were false converts. They wanted all the good things God promises without giving their lives to Him. George Whitfield said, "That is the reason we have so many mushroom converts," meaning when people hear of God's grace without first being convicted of His Law, converts pop up everywhere. Most people who claim to be Christian are mushrooms—they pop up with the first warmth of the sun, but shrivel up when it gets too hot—and the Law has never convicted them. But when we show individuals their sin by holding up the Ten Commandments, they are able to see themselves for what they truly are: sinners in need of a Savior. The use of the Law is supposed to draw them to the Savior, where they are able to find ultimate forgiveness.

I was right in the middle of teaching a course called "The Basic Training Course," a part of Kirk and Ray's ministry, during the time I crashed my plane. I missed two or three weeks of the class during my recovery time, but I started up again and finished it. I was still recuperating and had my cast on while I was teaching the class, and the whole church was pretty amazed—especially the first time I came hobbling in. It was as if I had been dead and was alive again. You should have seen their expressions when I walked in the door. Everyone was impressed that I had survived and that God had protected me.

Q: You seem to have a passion to share your faith. How did it begin?

Judy and I were on vacation in Florida and decided to go to Dr. D. James Kennedy's church one Sunday. I had always been impressed with the Coral Ridge ministry, the late Dr. D. James Kennedy's church, and their focus on the lost. The two things I think the Church should do are to equip the saints for the work of the ministry and to win the lost. As it turned out, Dr. Kennedy was not preaching that Sunday, which was disappointing. The fellow that filled in for him, though, was the director of "Evangelism Explosion" (EE), which was also the topic of his sermon. It was the first time I had heard about EE, but it got me very excited to use the method.

Back at my home church, I told Pastor Jim about EE and told him I wanted to go to a training session. Pastor Jim said, "I'll go with you." After we returned, I started teaching the classes at our church. We would go out mainly using the visitor cards from church, and knock on people's doors, and go through the EE presentation with them. I thought it was effective for that purpose, but it was just too long and too involved when meeting people on the streets. I knew that it had a function, but it was not really what I wanted long-term. But back to your question, I like what Ray Comfort says when he is asked the same question, "My passion to share the gospel began the moment I got saved!" And that was true for me as well.

When I saw Ray Comfort's television program *The Way of the Master*, I thought, "Oh, that is exactly what I am looking for!" Ray's teachings made so much sense and were very practical, as they were geared toward street evangelism, which is what I like to do.

My wife recently bought me the book *Promising Waters—Stories of Fishing and Following Jesus* by Jim Grassi. It has many stories and illustrations of "fishing" for the unsaved. The book starts out with a quote:

Among fishing instructors there is an adage often conveyed to new fisherman: "Ten percent of all fishermen catch 90 percent of the fish."

The successful fisherman properly prepares himself for the challenge. He consistently applies the knowledge and experience that make him an excellent angler (fisherman) every time he goes fishing.

Q: Have any of your pastors joined with you in the evangelism effort?

There was a church we attended several years ago, and when we first started attending, the church had only a couple of hundred people in attendance. The pastor was young and was very interested in outreach. He told me he was thinking of starting a bus ministry in order to reach out to the neighborhoods around the church. I told him I had been involved in a bus ministry before and how I thought we should do it. I made up a plan and the next thing I knew, I was in charge of it.

We called the bus ministry Kids' Club. Every Saturday I would go out to some of the lower end neighborhoods and knock on doors to invite kids to the church. If I saw kids out on the street, I would just start talking to them, asking where they lived and if their parents were home so that I could talk to them about Kids' Club.

Almost all of the kids I talked to the first year were skeptical, but eventually word spread to all the neighborhoods that Kids' Club was a lot of fun. The word was out on the street about what we were doing, so if we didn't pick someone up, they felt left out.

Every Saturday for years I would go out faithfully, invite kids, and give them a flyer that said what the services were about, when they started, and exactly what time the bus would pick them up. I always tried to get a commitment from the parents that their child would be ready. After I got the commitment, I wrote down the address. It usually took me five to six hours every Saturday to make the rounds, and then on Sunday we had Kids' Club.

Kids' Club evolved in different ways, but basically it was children's church. There was music and a mini-worship service that included puppets to keep the kids interested. After the service, we would provide snacks and hold a mini-Sunday school class. After Sunday school, it was time to drive them all home.

Our priority for every service was to make sure to present a clear gospel message. We always included a gospel presentation with a salvation message, being sure to include sin and its consequence. It was important to include sin and show how we all had offended God, so the kids would see why they must repent and turn to Christ.

When we first started Kids' Club, we had three or four adults involved. As the ministry grew, we had two buses and a couple of vans picking up the kids, and ended up with two hundred kids and about thirty adults ministering to them.

Because of Kids' Club, we had a lot of adults start coming to our church, and the church really grew. Some of the families had two adults living together, yet not married. Two couples were especially convicted of their sin, and got married in the church. The Kids' Club ministry was such a blessing in so many ways.

In fact, a couple of years ago I ran into a dad of one of the families, and asked him, "How are the kids doing?" He told me that one of his kids we had ministered to had gone to Bible school and become a full-time missionary. Wow! That really touched my heart, and made all the hard work worth it.

At my current church, Pastor Jim is very supportive of my evangelism efforts. He has required all of the pastors and staff to attend either "The Basic Training Course," or a one-day course I lead called "The Crash Course." Of course, Pastor Jim leads by example and has taken the course, too. Additionally, when I set up the evangelism booth at the local fairs, Pastor Jim and all the other pastors at our church are required to sign up to help man it for a few hours over the weekends. I'm sure that Pastor Jim's mandate helps to nudge them to help out and get involved, but once they are involved with the people, they seem to enjoy the experience and really get excited about sharing their faith and using the clever and entertaining assortment of *The Way of the Master* ice breaker tracts that we use.

Q: How do you respond when you are out on the streets and someone does not want to hear the gospel?

I simply move on. I know that God has those whose hearts will be opened, and that He will bring me to those that are ready to hear the Good News—those that have *good* soil. There are always plenty of people out there who are seeking and looking for answers, so why waste your time trying to convince people who do not care?

I heard some wise advice from Mark Spence, the dean of The Way of the Master's School of Biblical Evangelism. He said, "The next time you are rejected for the gospel's sake, or someone takes your tract and throws it in the trash, or maybe you are yelled at, do not get upset with the individual, but respond like a honey bee would. A honey bee does not sting the flower when it does not have pollen, it just moves on to the next flower to see if it can find pollen there."

So when I am having an unfruitful witnessing encounter, I try not to get upset and take it personally—or sting the individual. I simply move on to the next person, reminding myself that it is the message folks are rejecting, not me. Moreover, I am comforted by Jesus' words to the Christian:

> *Blessed are you when they revile and persecute you, and say all kinds of evil against you falsely for My sake. Rejoice and be exceedingly glad, for great is your reward in heaven, for so they persecuted the prophets who were before you.* (Matthew 5:11-12, NKJV)

Lastly, I remind myself of the words of Charles Spurgeon, Prince of Preachers:

> There is a door to each man's heart, and we have to find it, and enter it with the right key, which is to be found somewhere or other in the Word of God. All men are not to be reached in the same way, or by the same arguments, and as we are by all means to save some, we must be wise to win souls, wise with wisdom from above ... all the real power is in

the Lord's hands, and we must put ourselves fully at the disposal of the divine Worker, that He may work in us both to will and to do his good pleasure, so shall we by all means save some. (Ray Comfort, *Spurgeon Gold*, "The Sincerity of Prayer," Bridge-Logos Publishers, 71.)

I did not always think this way. At one point in my Christian walk, I thought that if the person did not get saved, then I had done something wrong. But within the last three to four years, many of Ray Comfort's teachings have opened my eyes to biblical evangelism and the fact that it is not my ability to convert souls—it is God's.

I still like to study apologetics in order to have more evidence to present, as it gives me a little more confidence, but I know that is not what is going to save people. God has His elect, and we evangelize as God's ordained means of finding them. I try to remember I am out on the streets for the ones that will be saved. I do not know who they are, so I preach to everyone. My wife says, "It is our job to show people the way, and the job of the Holy Spirit to save their souls." And that is where I find my rest. I know it is God's job to do the saving and my job to preach the gospel *biblically*. Time is short, so I have learned to spend my time sharing the gospel with folks who want to hear.

Q: *Do you ever experience a lack of passion for the lost or lose your focus on evangelism?*

I lost some of that passion during my early years because of my home life and all of the issues in my family that were going on while I was growing up. But I know that is not a good excuse. I guess deep down inside, I have never felt called to be in the ministry—full-time ministry—or to be a pastor.

Just this past Sunday, Pastor Jim asked, "Why do you come to church?" And then, "What is the purpose of the church?" People stood up and said, "To praise the Lord," and "For fellowship," and "For when we have needs, we can pray for each other." He did not call on me, but the theme on Sunday was "The Purpose of the Church." Basically, he preached on how God uses the local church to equip the saints for the work of the ministry and to save the lost, even if it is just one soul.

What Pastor Jim said reminded me of a quote from Canadian pastor, evangelist, and missionary supporter, Oswald J. Smith. Oswald, at one time, pastored the largest church in Canada and was known for preaching to crowds averaging 15,000 a night on one mission trip to Buenos Aires, Argentina. What he said strikes at the heart of what I believe:

> Oh, my friends, we are loaded with countless church activities, while the real work of the Church, that of evangelizing and winning the lost, is almost entirely neglected.

Honestly, there have been times when I am tired and I do not want to go out, but I go anyway. If I think about it, I do not really like people very much. But I know God loves them, and commands me to share my faith, and I do it because of my love for Him. It is not that I have a great love for people, but I have a great love for Him. He commands and I obey.

One good thing about the crash is it gave me a new witnessing tool. I made copies of the story I had written for the insurance company, added a cover page with a picture of the crash, and added more pictures at the end. I use the story like a tract and hand it out when I am witnessing to people who I think might be interested. Sometimes I talk to guys that do not seem very interested in talking about the Lord, so I hand a copy to them while asking, "Well, why don't you read this true story?"

Q: What gospel tract is your favorite?

I really like handing out Ray Comfort's *Million Dollar Bill* tract, but it really is hard to choose just one favorite, because all of his tracts are really good. The *Curved Illusion* is great too; everyone enjoys the trick it plays on the eyes. *Mind Game* is another very effective tract. I've even started sharing all of these at the county fair.

Curved Illusion is also printed in Spanish, and I find Hispanics really like this tract. I run into Hispanic folks everywhere. If they do not speak English, I will say, "*Qual es mas grande?*" which means, "Which one is bigger?" Since the tract is an illusion, they will point to the one they think is bigger, but they are always wrong. Then I hand the tract to them and point to the words on the back and they say, "*Gracias, gracias!*"

Q: Does your wife help you out on the streets when you share your faith?

Judy is a wonderful helper. The most important way she helps me is at home, taking care of the children and being a wonderful homemaker. This really frees *me* up to be able to share the gospel. When I know that our home is being managed well, I'm able to hit the streets regularly. Judy joins me and brings me snacks when I'm sharing the gospel. And if I need more tracts, she goes home and gets them. After our pastor's recent sermon, Judy leaned over and said, "You know, I think maybe I should take "The Way of the Master Evangelism Course" with you next time you teach it."

Q: What do you say to folks who are terrified to share their faith?

First, I tell them that they are like most Christians. In fact, I have met very few people who can honestly say, in any situation, they have no fear about sharing their faith. Welcome to the club. Second, I say that is why we have and teach *The Way of the Master* "Basic Training Course." Through the lessons, we learn that fear is good. It drives us to our knees to pray and rely on God's strength, not our own. And last, I remind people that we do not save people or give people salvation—only God through the Holy Spirit does that. We just have to do our part and inform people that there is an option as to where each of us will spend eternity—Heaven or hell.

The bottom line is, we have to ask ourselves the question: "Is my fear going to stop or inhibit me from potentially keeping people out of hell?" Loved ones, relatives, friends, or new acquaintances, they are all precious in God's eyes. In Ray Comfort's book *The Way of the Master*, he quotes Charles Spurgeon:

> The saving of souls, if a man has once gained love for perishing sinners and his blessed Master, will be an all-absorbing passion to him. It will so

carry him away, *that he will almost forget himself* in the saving of others. He will be like the brave fireman, who cares not for the scorch or the heat, so that he may rescue the poor creature on whom true humanity has set its heart. If sinners will be damned, at least let them leap to Hell over our bodies. And if they will perish, let them perish with our arms about their knees, imploring them to stay. If Hell must be filled, at least let it be filled in the teeth of our exertions, and let not one go there unwarned and unprayed for.

This aptly describes what I'm talking about.

Much of Ray Comfort and Kirk Cameron's ministry, The Way of the Master, is specifically directed to help all of us with fear issues and how to overcome them. The best teacher is experience—just getting out there and doing it. Their website, *www.wayofthemaster.com*, is filled with practical helps and encouragement. The next step to get powerful, on-the-job training is to attend their Ambassadors' Academy. The three-day seminar is mainly on-the-job training. Participants will see others sharing their faith through one-on-one encounters, in open-air preaching, and on busy intersections doing forty-five-second "stoplight preaching." Participants have ample opportunity to test the waters and overcome their fears.

Q: Is there a book besides the Bible that has been an encouragement to you?

I have really enjoyed *Spurgeon Gold*, compiled by Ray Comfort. It has some of the best quotes on evangelism and living for Christ I have ever read. They have convicted my heart and stirred me in my personal walk with the Lord, challenging me to share my faith—while I still have the time and strength to do it. Some of my favorite quotes from the book are:

Have you no wish for others to be saved? Then you are not saved yourself. Be sure of that.

God commands each Christian to go out into the world and share the gospel. He does not suggest sharing your faith.

* * *

Let every man understand that he will never have remission of sin while he is in love with sin, and that if he abides in sin, he cannot obtain the pardon of sin. There must be a hatred of sin, a loathing of it, and a turning from it, or it is not blotted out.

Unfortunately, especially America, we use a comparison to others in determining our own goodness. Well, I'm not as bad as so-and-so and I go to church. Not recognizing that sin is sin in God's eyes. He is looking for a Church that is as white as snow—unblemished. If I read the Bible correctly, God does not weigh the sin of one lie as any less of a sin than one murder or even multiple murders. We need to realize that God's judgment is for all of us. We have to turn away from every form of ungodliness.

* * *

Whatever I believe or do not believe, the command to love my neighbor as myself still retains its claim upon me, and God forbid that any views or opinions should so contract my soul and harden my heart as to make me forget this law of love! The love of God is first, but this by no means lessens the obligation of love to man; in fact, the first command includes the second. We are to seek our neighbor's conversion because we love him.

This is a tough one for me because I often struggle with the thought of loving all of my fellow man. I get more and more impatient with people who, in arrogance, reject the gospel and think they have all of these intellectual arguments to prove their position. I just want to say to them, "Just go to hell, then. It's your choice; my hands are clean." Of course, God loves all men and wants everyone to come to His saving grace, and all I can do is make the offer.

* * *

Remember again, what it is you are trifling with. It is your own soul, the soul that can never die.... Now if you must play the fool, find something cheaper to play with than this.

This is my point exactly for those who reject the gospel message as mentioned above. They have no clue as to what they are trifling with.

* * *

Herein is the folly of so many Christians— that, being wrapped up in the interest of their own salvation, and taken up with their own doubts and fears, they feel little care and they take little trouble for others. They never seem to empty themselves out into the world that is around them, and never seem to get into a world bigger than the homestead in which they live. But when a man begins to think about others, to care for others, to value the souls of others, then his thoughts of God get larger.

I have found this to be true throughout my life. When I focus on myself, things only get worse, but when I reach out to others, my problems seem smaller. Many times I just do not have the energy and ambition to witness or minister, but because I have made a commitment to God and to others to be there—the booth, the class, etc.,—I feel obligated and show up. Invariably before the day is out, I'm refreshed, excited, and feel I got more out of the experience than I gave.

* * *

Save some, O Christians! By all means, save some. From yonder flames and outer darkness, and the weeping, wailing, and gnashing of teeth, seek to save some! Let this, as in the case of the apostle, be your great, ruling object in life: that by all means, you might save some

Fire away, brethren! You do not know where your shot will strike, but "there is a billet for every bullet."

Both of the above quotes are part of my witnessing credo. If I don't go out, I am guaranteed that I am not helping anyone escape the depths and torment of hell. But every time I try and make the attempt, some might be saved.

That is all God asks me to do. By faith, try—the rest is up to Him.

* * *

Unless we deny ourselves and lay violent hands upon the impulses of our nature, we shall never come to the place where the crowns are distributed to the conquerors.

Avoiding sin takes work and diligence. Our nature is sinful and all things naturally gravitate toward destruction. It takes purposeful thought and effort to avoid falling into one of Satan's lies. Without reading the Word of God and using it as your sword, as a weapon to defeat sin, our nature will destroy us.

* * *

This is one of the first works of the Law—to show us what spotless purity it demands, and to reveal to us the matchless perfection, which alone can meet its requirements.

God's expectations are high when it comes to sin—we should be guilty of none. The Law makes it very clear. We tend to minimize sin and focus on God's grace. I hope that when the trumpet sounds, I am wrong and shown to be too legalistic. Otherwise, if I am right, many are going to be very disappointed when God's judgment rules the land.

* * *

Do you want to be saved by your own righteousness? Do you know what kind of righteousness it must be?... When a man commits one sin, he is guilty of disobedience to all the commandments of God, for "he that offends in one point is guilty of all." Here is a chain containing twenty links. If I break one of them, I have broken the chain.

This is a great visual to see what the Scripture indicates. No sin has any more weight than another. Breaking any of the Ten Commandments is like violating them all. We seem to think God will view murder as evil and deserving of hell, but a lie now and again is only a slight indiscretion.

* * *

If a father and mother pray for their children, but never pray with them, or to speak to them personally about the welfare of their souls, they must not wonder if they are not brought to Christ.

Our primary goal as parents should be to lead our children to Christ. We cannot leave this up to Sunday school teachers and our pastors. They should be able to assist in our efforts, but ultimately it is our responsibility.

* * *

When once God the Holy Spirit applies the Law to the conscience, secret sins are dragged to light; little sins are magnified to their true size; and things apparently harmless become exceedingly sinful. Before that dread Searcher of the hearts and Trier of the reins makes His entrance into the soul, it appears righteous, just, lovely, and holy; but when He reveals the hidden evils, the scene is changed. Offenses, which were once styled peccadilloes, trifles, freaks of youth, follies, indulgences, little slips, etc., then appear in their true colors, as breaches of the Law of God, deserving condign punishment.

God will give us every opportunity to ask for forgiveness of sin throughout our lives, until our last breath, when we cross to the other side of life to death—that is God's grace.

* * *

The day of death is the beginning of our best days.

My mom had requested that we put a large fork in her hand for everyone to see during her open-casket viewing at her funeral. She received the idea from a book she had recently read. She wanted to have a large fork in her hand so every one would ask, "What is that for?" Our response was to be, "Because the best is yet to come." At many of the church potlucks, an announcement would be made: "Hang onto your forks—dessert is now being served. The best is yet to come." As a Christian, that is our hope.

* * *

You cannot preach conviction of sin unless you have suffered it. You cannot preach faith unless you have practiced it. You cannot preach faith unless you have exercised it. You may talk about these things, but there will be no power in the talk unless what is said has been experimentally proved in your own soul.

Experience is the best teacher and often the best witness. It is very difficult to have true empathy for people and their circumstances if you have not personally walked in their shoes.

* * *

I do not think we ever pray with such fervor of supplication in our prosperity as we do in our adversity. And then how precious the promises become! As we only see the stars when the shadows gather at night, so the promises shine out like newly kindled stars when we get into the night of affliction. I am sure that there are passages of Scripture, which are full of consolation the depths of which we do not even imagine yet, and we never shall know all that is in them till we get into the depths of soul trouble, which correspond with them. There are points of view from which scenery is to be beheld at its best; and, until we find out those points of view, we may be missing the sight of some of the most beautiful objects in nature. God leads us one way and another by our chastisements to understand and prize His promises. And, oh, dear friends, how should we ever know the faithfulness of God if it were not for affliction? We might talk about it and theoretically understand it; but to try to prove the greatness of Jehovah's love—this comes not except by the way of affliction and trial.

A good dose of trials and tribulations will determine if you trust God or not. Are you a false convert? Many times the presence of God and His accompanying peace will only be experienced to their fullest at the height of a great storm.

* * *

If you will not have death unto sin, you shall have sin unto death. There is no alternative, if you do not die to sin, you shall die for sin. If you do not slay sin, sin will slay you.

Satan has been around longer than man, and knows man's weakness better then man knows himself. Satan has thousands of years of experience. His goal is the death and destruction of man. He is the master of lies and has learned to convince us that sin for a season will not hurt; there is always time to repent. But he knows there are no guarantees for how many days we will be breathing air on this Earth. His goal is physical and spiritual death. Can you afford to play the one-more-day game?

—————■—————

Another great book and help for witnessing is Mark Cahill's *One Thing You Can't Do in Heaven.* For instance, he uses this statement as a lead-in to witnessing: "Do you realize there is a 100 percent chance you will die?" Then he adds, "and do you realize that you will be dead a whole lot longer than you will be alive?" I have used that thought many times to get a conversation going about a person's eternal destiny.

He also has a summary of some very useful questions to use when you get often-used objections to the gospel. The questions are structured to help show people they really can't defend their positions. Often, they are just repeating things they have heard, but have no real facts or knowledge of themselves. Ask people these questions: (1) What do you mean by that? (2) How do you know that to be true? (3) Where do you get your information? And the big one— (4) What if you are wrong?

Q: *What are some of your favorite sayings?*

I like to write notes in my Bible. Others might prefer not to, but I've found it helpful through the years. I've written sermon notes in the margins of my Bible over the years, and have some favorites:

Are the things you are living for worth Christ dying for?

* * *

Do not look back, else the devil will gain on you. Keep your eyes straight ahead to Jesus. (See Luke 9:59-62; 1 John 1:7-9.)

* * *

God does not make mistakes!

* * *

It is more important *who* is in your boat, than *what* is in your boat.

* * *

All sunshine makes a desert.

* * *

The sun is always shining above the storm.

* * *

It is not the circumstances of life that shape you; it is your response to the circumstances that shapes you.

* * *

The outcome of your life will be determined by the choices you make, not by the dreams you have or the goals you set.

* * *

Make sure you are investing your life, time, and resources in things that are lasting and have eternal value, not in things that pass away.

* * *

God does not change, but He does *move*.

* * *

Life is not a sprint—it is a marathon. You can stumble and fall and still have the opportunity to finish and win the race. In the hundred-yard dash, one stumble or false move and the race is over; you lose. Not in a marathon.

* * *

Do not limit God. All things are possible with Him. What man cannot do, God can.

* * *

The bigger the cross you are packing, the bigger the works that will come.

* * *

Bigger cross = bigger works = bigger *heavenly* rewards.

I wrote the above next to the following passage in Luke 14:27-35, NASB:

> Whoever does not carry his own cross and come after Me cannot be My disciple. For which one of you, when he wants to build a tower, does not first sit down and calculate the cost to see if he has enough to complete it? Otherwise, when he has laid a foundation, and is not able to finish, all who observe it begin to ridicule him, saying, "This man began to build and was not able to finish." Or what king, when he sets out to meet another king in battle, will not first sit down and take counsel whether he is strong enough with ten thousand men to encounter the one coming against him with twenty thousand? Or else, while the other is still far away, he sends a delegation and asks terms of peace. So therefore, no one of you can be My disciple who does not give up all his own possessions. Therefore, salt is good; but if even salt has become tasteless, with what will it be seasoned? It is useless either for the soil or for the manure pile; it is thrown out. He who has ears to hear, let him hear.

* * *

If you do the same thing, you'll get the same outcome. If you want a different outcome, something must change.

* * *

Definition of *insanity*: Doing the same thing over and over and expecting a different outcome.

* * *

Anything can change if God is at the center. When the only answer is God, the outcome is always a miracle, and God gets the glory.

* * *